LEGENDS & LORE
OF
NEW BRUNSWICK

LEGENDS & LORE

OF

NEW BRUNSWICK

MARK NEUROHR-PIERPAOLI

THE
History
PRESS

Published by The History Press
Charleston, SC
www.historypress.com

First published 2024

Manufactured in the United States

ISBN 9781467157988

Library of Congress Control Number: 2024938210

For my family.

CONTENTS

PREFACE

As a high school teacher of both history and English, I've come to appreciate how different methods from each of my subjects complement the accessibility and delivery of content in the other. Good storytelling makes history come alive. A creative take and an engaging voice somehow makes historical material feel more tangible and less foreign despite the decades separating us from our sources.

Likewise, true historical facts resonate with audiences. Authors who use accurate details and tell "real" stories make the incredible feel more authentic and believable, even if the text is a complete work of fiction.

When I attended Rutgers (largely because I'd heard tell the legends of grease trucks serving fat sandwiches through all hours of the night), I fell in love with New Brunswick in a way that many of its transient college residents never do. I decided to stick around after graduating from "the banks of the Old Raritan" and work locally.

My first teaching job was at New Brunswick High School, and I remained there for more than a decade. In my years living and working in the city, I moved around a lot from one neighborhood to another. With each jump, I learned to get my bearings and feel the rhythms of daily life in a new section of the city. It was during this time that I gained a fuller appreciation for the many different moving parts of New Brunswick.

In the areas surrounding Rutgers, there wasn't much activity until the early afternoon, when the neighborhood finally started to wake up. It was often busiest around two or three o'clock in the morning as the bars, parties and underground music venues (literal basements in residential "show houses") let out.

Around the hospitals, traffic congestion was unavoidable during my commute. Countless hours were spent wishing I'd taken a different route.

Downtown, the drinks-after-work crowd slowly changed composition until it became the nighttime-locals crowd out for a pint or two.

The 'hoods where most of my students lived had some of the most authentic and delicious regional cuisine outside of the countries where they originated.

In every pocket of New Brunswick, the people who called it home shared their firsthand and secondhand and even thirdhand knowledge of the history of the city. I've since come to learn that much of what they told me was surprisingly accurate.

When I moved away, I still felt somehow that my story in the city had not yet ended. Soon, I started a small company leading haunted history tours in the downtown business districts of various walkable New Jersey towns. It was an entrepreneurial and somewhat romantic idea that emerged from my own travel experiences.

Wherever I went, I enlisted the services of a local tour guide. Invariably, my tourist experience was heightened through their local knowledge and friendly expertise. I wanted to do the same for others. Plus, I always saw them doing well in tips!

In all honesty, it was a bit of a dream to have people willingly pay me to learn the knowledge and stories I'd gleaned in my years of toil studying history's mysteries. This was in direct contrast, of course, to the captive but hardly captivated audiences I'd been nurturing in the public schools.

Within a few years, I reached a decision to expand the tours to New Brunswick. It was natural given my connection to the place. Plus, my team was largely composed of other educators with ties to the area who I'd befriended during my time here.

However, I was surprised to realize that despite its extensive history, there were no "ghost books" set in New Brunswick like there were in all the other towns where we operated. The wide body of literature that had blossomed in recent years under the umbrella of the local legends, folklore and ghost stories genre—rife with tales passed down through the ages—had somehow passed over New Brunswick. Thus, the necessity of writing this little book became evident. There could be no tour without the prerequisite source material.

In the stories I've collected here, I've attempted to blend my two domains by coupling engaging storytelling with fantastic but true history. I sincerely thank anyone holding this copy for giving the material a chance.

If you enjoy what you read, I encourage you to take a walking tour that highlights and features the places and stories you'll encounter in these pages. Tracing its steps through the nooks and crannies of local history with a friendly guide will help to bring its magic to life.

ACKNOWLEDGEMENTS

I'd like to offer thanks and gratitude to everyone who has helped bring this book to fruition. First, to my wife, Sarah Siering, without whose love, support and partnership I could not have completed this endeavor (or any of the other ones). To my daughters, Eve and Eleanor, whose joy, curiosity and wonderful questions are an inspiration. To the rest of my family, especially my mother, Kathleen Neurohr; my father, Alessandro Pierpaoli; and my brother, Adam Neurohr-Pierpaoli, whose advice (solicited or not) has always been useful and sound. To the instrumental team at Local Walking Tours, who I'm so proud to work alongside, especially Liz Sheridan and Sarah Neiderman. You are really lovely people. To all my friends who read through drafts, including Rob Cottignies, thank you for your time, wisdom and encouragement, and especially Ruth Yeselson, for first teaching me how to write a great paragraph. To the people at Arcadia Publishing and The History Press, whose belief in the project made it real, and especially Banks Smither, whose guidance and insights were critically important, and Laurie Krill, who guided the project to its completion. To the fantastic librarians at the New Brunswick Free Public Library and the Rutgers University Libraries for their diligence in helping to locate some very obscure references and their work to scan photographs, including Drue Williamson, and especially Bob Belvin and Christine Lutz, for their assistance with photos and additional research. To all the writers, educators, creators, historians, researchers and investigators whose broad shoulders have provided such firm footing, including Eric Mintel, Elizabeth Ciccone, Jessica Shea, Ray Brennan and Mimi Omiecinski, and especially Ann Alvarez, whose hypothesis and research forms most of the basis of the hidden treasure chapter. To the readers, whose audience supports continuing works in this genre. Finally, to the people of New Brunswick, whose stories deserve to be told.

INTRODUCTION

New Brunswick, New Jersey, has gone by many names: Ahanderamock, Inian's Ferry, Prigmore's Swamp, Hub City, Greater Rutgers, The Health Care City and Nueva Brunswick. No matter what you call it, though, this is a place with many moving parts. The borders of its vibrant neighborhoods overlap. Its diverse communities intersect in unexpected ways.

Creative, hardworking people fill the houses and streets here. They embrace the melting pot of cultures mixing within city limits, adding their own flavors with personal stories and perspectives. One generation passes down the story of this place to the next as much through informal means as through academia.

New Brunswick retains important vestiges from the past, and yet it proves to be an ever changing landscape and skyline. The hustle and bustle of centuries reverberate throughout New Brunswick. It goes back thousands of years to the Indigenous people who first blazed trails here. Their paths became the railways and highways, with all roads leading back to the city like the spokes of a hubcap.

The flooding waters of the Raritan River provided important access to the region. European settlers established settlements on its banks that transformed into dense urban centers. Shipping thrived, and economic opportunities brought droves of new arrivals. The city today teems with people from around the world.

The early industriousness of a few men and women gave rise to corporate industrial headquarters that continue to spur growth. The incoming and outgoing university students who form the ever-flowing lifeblood of the city continue to fuel the city's changes.

Many have come and gone. Sometimes, the ones who live here, the ones who were born here and sometimes the ones who arrive here, decide to stay here. And some never, ever leave.

New Brunswick is a city of lost history. So many changes have taken place in such a relatively short span of time that many of the physical remnants of the past have been destroyed.

People continue to write the story of its future though. In a storied place like this, tales from long ago tend to disappear only to reanimate again in new retellings. Perhaps in places where no one expected them to surface. Perhaps in times distantly removed from the source.

Stories swept under the rug have a way of popping back up again. Whispers and mutters remind us that nothing remains unspeakable forever. The passage of time reveals hidden histories. Macabre motives become uncovered like bones poking from a shallow grave.

Wiping away the dust of the past reveals obscured truths. New light sheds new life on the same old stories over and over again. These tales become legends that take on new meaning.

This book attempts to investigate the nuggets of hidden truth and the shadowy recesses of institutional memories that spawn local lore and urban legends. Primary sources are referenced whenever possible. The search of historical records, interviews with experts and combing through old newspapers have dredged facts and fictions alike to the surface for the reader's examination. The author alone assumes responsibility for any errors or omissions.

The stories within contain true history woven throughout with unverifiable hearsay. To that end, the historical aspects of the narratives within are accurate to a reasonably high degree. As for the folklore, legends and hauntings, readers will decide for themselves what to believe.

LEGENDS OF
THE FIRST PEOPLE

To know a place, one must first know the lay of the land. In New Brunswick, New Jersey, that understanding begins with the winding bends of the Raritan River. This muddy waterway originates from two smaller converging river branches that stream together in the hills of Somerset County. From there, the Raritan runs southeast, carving through the red shales and sandstones of Central Jersey. It flows across Middlesex County before finally emptying into the Raritan Bay at the Atlantic Ocean.

There is a point where the Raritan becomes tidal and laps its shorelines at higher or lower points depending on the time of day. The rising and falling ebbs of the water here may have helped the river earn its name. *Raritan* could be derived from an Indigenous term meaning "stream overflows."

The land the river runs through was first inhabited by the Lenni Lenape Tribe, the earliest known population to live in New Jersey. Lenape use of the land dates back centuries before the arrival of Europeans. Some estimates date Lenape arrival back to the thaw of the last ice age, some ten thousand to thirteen thousand years ago.

Tribes like the Lenni Lenape were organized by their regionally distinct cognate languages. Speakers of the Algonquian dialectical family of languages stretched from modern-day Canada down through New England and along the Mid-Atlantic coast.

By the 1600s, the tract of land south of the Raritan where New Brunswick stands today was a swampy cedar forest. Long before it was called New Brunswick, though, a village named Ahanderamock stood along the banks of the Raritan.

The people in Ahanderamock would have utilized natural resources to build their homes. In this region, Native Americans lived in single-doorway, single-family wooden huts called wigwams. Several families may have dwelt in much larger longhouses.

Ahanderamock was a fairly settled village. There are references to adjacent burial grounds, although the locations cannot be verified. Traditionally, however, such cemeteries were placed on the east side of a hill, close to the water.

High population density was not always a defining feature of New Jersey. Upon first European contact, conservative estimates suggest that there were fewer than ten thousand Indigenous people living on the Jersey peninsula.

The Naraticons were the first known subtribe of the Lenni Lenape to settle in the Raritan Valley. They resided north of the river, a natural boundary with Ahanderamock to the south. It's somewhat difficult to determine which subtribes resided farther south and what languages were spoken. This is

Opposite: The original deed exchanging land below the Raritan for a list of goods from Native Americans to European settlers in 1681. *Image of public document from the New Jersey State Archives.*

Left: Lenape women Jennie Bobb and her daughter Nellie Longhat, taken in Oklahoma, 1915. Descendants of the Lenni Lenapes are often located much farther west than New Jersey. *Public domain photo from the National Anthropological Archives, Smithsonian Institution, Washington, via Wikimedia Commons.*

due to Ahanderamock's unique position sandwiched between more defined parts to the north and south.

People here may have spoken Munsee, the language commonly used by Lenapes to the north. In fact, *Ahanderamock* was a Munsee word. Or perhaps they spoke Unalachtigo, a Lenape dialect associated with the central part of Lenape territory. The record of the Unalachtigo language is incomplete though.

It may have even been a dialect or strongly accented version of Unami, the more widely spoken Lenape language to the south. Regardless of the languages they spoke, however, the Lenni Lenape were the first to live, worship, die and be buried in Ahanderamock.

In 1681, a small group of Native Americans led by one named Escharck signed a deed exchanging title for the land surrounding Ahanderamock to a group of English settlers. Escharck and his companions were likely unfamiliar with the English system of landownership. According to the original deed stored in the New Jersey's State Archives, five-hundred-acre lots in the conveyance of more than ten thousand acres (or more than fifteen square miles) were bartered away in exchange for a grocery list of items that included:

> *200 fathem of White Wampem, ten blankets, 20 Duffeild Coates, 10 Guns and 12 Kettles whereof two of them 8 Gallons a.p. [apeice], 26 yards Stroud Waters, 25 axes and 20 paire of Stockings, 20 Shirts and 5 made Coats, 4 pistolls and 60 Barrs Lead, half a Barrell of powder, 25 paire Tobacco tongs, 2 Ankers of Rum, 2 half Fatts of beer, 1/2 anker Mollasses, a tramel and 60 knives, 20 tobacco boxes, 25 to Shot, 1/2 a [illegible] of bread.*

The Lenapes may have been under the impression that the exchange was a gift for temporary use of the land, as was a custom among Native people who shared resources. Folklore alternately suggests that they ultimately relinquished their claims here because they believed the area to be cursed and uninhabitable in the first place.

In time, as Indigenous people transferred more land to settlers throughout the 1600s, colonial development increased. In the four hundred years since then, displacement, disease and violence have greatly reduced the Native populations of North America.

However, the Lenni Lenape tribe has not disappeared. Their diaspora spreads across the nation today, with descendants mostly located in Oklahoma or Wisconsin.

Beliefs and Customs

There are gaps in the extant knowledge of the language and history of the Lenape people. Fortunately, a number of stories exist through oral tradition. The Lenni Lenape are a proud tribe, known as the eldest people and respectfully accorded the title "grandfathers" among other Algonquian tribes. The legends that the descendants pass down may be some of the oldest on record in North America.

As in many cultures, tribe members tell traditional stories for a variety of purposes. Many describe spiritual beliefs. Others warn of danger or attempt to tell the future through prophecy. Stories lend insight into practices, customs and behaviors. Some exist to simply terrify children into behaving!

Mising'w mask formerly on display in a Lenape exhibit at the Paterson Museum. *Photo by Mark Neurohr-Pierpaoli, courtesy of the Paterson Museum, Paterson, New Jersey.*

A number of myths and legends about frighteningly powerful deities and mischievous wilderness creatures survive. They also maintain stories and beliefs about ghosts and spirits. Their stories may have even influenced the folk tales of colonial settlers who came after.

The Lenapes believe that a divine Creator god named Kitanitowit is responsible for the creation of everything. There is also a pantheon of deities who reside in the natural world. These figures are responsible for the forces and elements of life and nature.

Perhaps the most important figure is Mising'w, the Lenape Mask Spirit. He is a sacred entity who balances nature with the human impact on it. In most depictions, Mising'w's supernatural face is colored half red and half black.

In the legend of Mising'w's origins, the animals of the forest learn that the Great Spirit intends to create humans. They beseech the deity Mising'w to speak to Kitanitowit on their behalf. The creatures fear that people will dig up the earth, chop the trees and pollute the rivers and air. Mising'w agrees with the animals, and so he goes forth.

He knows enough not to question the Creator, so he does not ask the reason why humans are necessary. Instead, he simply requests that the Creator change his plans and not bother to create people at all. The Creator agrees to settle the dispute with a contest. Whoever can move a mountain farther shall win the argument and have their way. Mising'w goes first and tries to pick up the mountain, but he fails to move it an inch. The Creator then pushes the mountain so forcefully that it smashes Mising'w in the face and disfigures the spirit.

Realizing his offense, the injured Mising'w begs the Creator's forgiveness and tries to mend the situation. He asks to serve the Creator's will by protecting the deer of the forest for people to use. The Creator grants this wish, and this becomes his role.

The Lenape people describe Mising'w as taking the form of a large man whose body is covered with long, dark hair. The red and black "Living Solid Face" is large and round. He rides through the woods on the back of a deer. A protective guardian of the forest, he assists those who respect the forest but punishes those who destroy it.

He is also said to look after children. In one tale, Mising'w appears to three boys. He takes them on a strange journey through the sky to his home and promises them help into the future. Years later, earthquakes disrupt the lives of the Lenapes. Mising'w returns with instructions for the three same boys, now men, to carve a mask in his likeness. He describes the method to properly use the mask in order to save the world.

Named Xinkwikàn, the ritual requires tools including a turtle shell rattle, a bag and a staff. Recitations of dreams and visions of power are repeated at an annual ceremony, and a dance is held. Great calamity will continue to befall the people if they should ever lose this tradition.

Mising'w statue, no longer on display. *Photo by Mark Neurohr-Pierpaoli, courtesy of the Paterson Museum, Paterson, New Jersey.*

The Mask Ceremony pays respect to Mising'w on an annual basis. In the days leading up to this event, a responsible tribe member who stores and keeps a Mising'w mask safe throughout the year takes it out. Around the full moon of May, this person dons the iconic red and black face and wears a full bearskin costume so that no part of his body is visible.

M.R. Harrington, a writer and curator at the Museum of the American Indian in the early twentieth century, described the creature as having a "hideous appearance." The costumed Mising'w impersonator rides around to all the Lenape houses to let everyone know that the time for the ritual is at hand, and the people give him gifts of tobacco, which he stashes away in a bag and kicks the dirt in thanks. The haunting creature never speaks.

As he travels from one home to another, disobedient children learn that this terrifying entity will carry them away in a sack full of snakes if they continue to misbehave. Understandably, they try not to incur the wrath of their parents while standing in the presence of the unsettling figure. Harington notes that whenever the Mising'w impersonator is summoned, it does not take long to frighten the weakness, sickness or laziness out of the kids.

Mising'w is not the only monstrous figure in their traditions. Other Lenni Lenape folktales involve the Wemategunis, a kind of forest gremlin that haunts the wilderness. These spritely magical figures resemble the stories of fairies or elves across many cultures.

The Wemategunis are dwarf-like creatures about waist high. They play mean pranks, but they also appreciate when someone abides their antics with good humor. Wemategunis may intervene in human affairs to set their wrongs right again. Children were accustomed to searching in the sand for the tracks of these little people while playing at the beach.

The Lenni Lenape people wisely fear and respect the Wemategunis. When provoked, the Wemategunis could use their strange and ample powers to create mischief and mayhem. One legend of the Wemategunis involves a hunter who separated from his companions to track a deer. He stalked the animal for some distance before successfully achieving the kill. He picked up and carried the carcass to return to his group but found himself lost in unfamiliar surroundings.

While he tried to find his way, a mocking voice began to call to him. Still carrying the deer, the hunter crisscrossed a valley trying to find the source of the voice. It was always just beyond his search. "Over here!" cried the voice, and the hunter would switch directions. "No, over here!" it called, coming from the way he'd already been.

Finally, he threw down the deer and rushed headlong toward the sound of the voice and encountered a laughing Wemategunis. The imp wanted to see how long the hunter would endure his taunts without dropping the heavy animal.

Another legend of the Wemategunis relates the sad tale of a gambler with beautiful eyes who unfairly charms other players out of their money. He courts the envy of the great chief of gamblers who lives on the moon. The spirit comes to earth and wins the gambler's eyes in a contest, leaving him blind and friendless. Years later, the accursed man encounters a Wemategunis but, unable to see, mistakes the creature for a child.

The elf offers to venture to the moon on behalf of the man to retrieve his eyes. The favor, however, is premised on the condition that the man can no longer gamble or beguile others. Instead, he must use his attractiveness for the benefit of the community.

The man agrees, the Wemategunis keeps its word and, in a happy ending, the reformed gambler follows through on his promises.

DEATH AND THE AFTERLIFE

In addition to their legends and folktales, Lenapes engage in performative religious rituals around deaths, funerals and burials. The belief in unseen forces, the afterlife and ghosts holds a special place in Lenni Lenape culture. Perhaps the most important feature of the spiritual world manifests in powerful dreams or visions. This is the main conduit of communication between the supernatural realm and the physical world.

Historically, as young boys about twelve years old entered adolescence, they could begin their quest to identify a spirit protector. Although not everyone was blessed with a guardian of this sort, to have one meant to always have the favor of a friend beyond the physical world. This power would take a close personal interest in the boy for the rest of his life.

Contact with such a spirit could be induced by fasting, often in the form of traveling alone through the forest without food for twelve days. This was paired with rough treatment by his elders or medicines that induced vomiting. A spirit might be moved to take pity on the poor boy and come to visit him in a fevered dream.

This vision would often begin as a man or an ancestor, but finally the spirit would turn and reveal its true self in the form of an animal. The story of the encounter with the vision would be repeated at the annual Xinkwikàn (Big House) ceremony.

The Lenape believed that these ever-present spirits in the world were called *manetu* and could affect the lives of people. On the one hand, they put plenty of effort into inviting good spirits into their lives and keeping them at peace. Personal pendants worn around the neck represented guardian spirits. They offered the manetu gifts like flowers and tobacco pipes. Ceremonies honored them as well. Such ceremonies celebrated events like weddings, births, successful hunts and harvests.

Manetuwak on the other hand were evil spirits or monsters. They believed that Great Horned Serpents, a Giant Bear and other monsters that dwelled in the water brought evil. While a medicine could be made from the tooth of such a creature to heal wounds, the Lenape also believed that these supernatural forces were the cause of any sickness that led to death. They worked just as hard to keep the manetuwak at bay. Indeed, offending the spirits by performing ceremonies incorrectly invited the harmful spirits to cause illness. Thus, religious routines carried grave significance.

Despite their best efforts to thwart disease, early death was not uncommon for Lenapes in the sixteenth and seventeenth centuries. Many did not live past their forties. Naming children was not typical until they were three years old due to the high rate of child mortality.

Archaeological and anthropological research suggests that some people had graves lined with tree bark or dried grass and other plants. Others were provided coffins. Those preparing the burial would carve a notch in the coffin and mark it with red paint. This allowed the spirit of the deceased to come and go as necessary.

Traditional rites dictated how to bury dead people. The head faced east, with legs bent close to the body and arms folded across the chest. Mourners placed a wooden marker at the grave and lit a ceremonial fire for the deceased to take with them. This would keep them warm on their journey.

The dead wore ceremonial clothes prepared during life and were interred with personal items. Men were buried with tools carved from antlers, for instance, or children with spoons and bird-shaped pendants. A number of women have been found buried with two pipes, but the significance of this remains a mystery.

Modern accounts of their religious practices demonstrate some of the beliefs of the Lenni Lenapes toward the end of life. Upon death, several days of customary ceremonies follow. This includes a wake that lasts all night and funeral feasts. One year of mourning ensues.

The Lenni Lenape continue to hold certain beliefs regarding death and the separation of the body from the *lenapeokan*, or the soul. The soul leaves the body at the moment when the heart stops. This is what Lenapes refer to as death.

Just prior to death, the lenapeokan can leave the body and travel around visiting people and places. After twelve days of ascension, these souls may go to live with Kitanitowit, the Creator spirit, in the twelfth and highest heaven.

The place where this Great Spirit lives is like here on earth, but everything is easygoing and without annoyance, worries or responsibility. In this happy place, the ancestors are waiting to greet the newcomers.

After the introduction of Christianity, the idea of an evil force counterweight to the Great Spirit was introduced into Lenape beliefs. Originally, it was suggested that people who behaved badly in life may not enter the happy place and must watch from the outside, excluded at a distance. This was not exactly a punishment, per se, but rather a way to keep the inhabitants of the inside community happy.

Eventually, the idea was introduced that these unfortunate souls may go to live where the evil spirit Mahtantu resides instead. There, stinging and biting insects torment the deceased. They will eventually become insects themselves and are finally sent back to earth by Mahtantu to irritate people.

This resonates with modern Lenape stories about ghosts and spirits that bother the living. Starting a project that remains unfinished at the time of death may delay a spirit's journey to either destination. This spirit will try to come back to finish the job, but this inevitably upsets people. They will hear his noises and feel his spirit around.

It is also claimed that wandering ghosts may lay traps by throwing an object onto a path. Whoever goes over it is bewitched and will become sick or injured.

Not all ghosts are malevolent though. Some Lenapes claim to have been given blessings, dreams or visions by ghosts and as such claim the ghosts as their guardian spirits throughout life.

At certain times, a meeting held at a burial ground could allow someone with such a protector to communicate with the dead. James Wolf was one man who held such power. M.R. Harrington describes the story of how one time a man was drowned, and the body could not be located. Wolf used his gifts and "walked up and down the river-banks, with a companion, talking to the water. At last a strange sound was heard." He stopped and said that noise was the spirit of the dead man, and he pointed to a nearby spot in the water. There, the body was finally found wedged beneath a sunken log in a hole below the water.

A DIFFERENT WORLD

The world that the ancient Indigenous populations inhabited has significantly changed. However, the Lenni Lenape have survived into the modern era, and the stories and beliefs of their ancestors provide insight into the way of life in villages like Ahanderamock, the tract of land to the south of the Raritan that would one day become New Brunswick.

Although the full stories of Native Americans like Escharck and his companions who granted deeds to the first settlers of New Brunswick cannot be known, it is possible to gain insight into their customs and traditions through both the historical record and modern accounts of the legends and religious rituals that are still being passed down today.

Given the history of the changes in ownership of the land, it's no wonder that the city that was settled on the Lenni Lenape village of Ahanderamock remains the site of so many unsettling haunting legends and folktales to this day.

PIRATES, PATRIOTS AND HIDDEN TREASURE

The story of New Brunswick is full of caves, tunnels and mines whose entrances have been lost or destroyed. Secret passages that lead to the Raritan from homes along the river and even from the frat houses on College Avenue suggest that smuggling operations from the water have existed at various points. Sealed and boarded-up Prohibition era tunnels connecting the basements of houses and businesses in various neighborhoods still exist in different parts of the city. Historical references to a copper mine with a rich vein of ore are coupled with the legend of a hidden entrance somewhere in the vicinity of modern-day Mine Street. All of this is to say that if someone at some point wished to hide a significant quantity of treasure, it's just as likely to have remained hidden to this day as it is to have already been found.

THE GOLDEN AGE OF PIRACY

In the 1600s, New Jersey was split in two by a haphazard survey line that demarcated East Jersey from West Jersey, two distinct colonies at the time thanks to the political whims of the earliest proprietors. The somewhat arbitrary boundary was erased when "the Jerseys" unified in 1702 at the command of Queen Anne, but subsequent attempts to correct the original line occurred in the 1700s. The cultural and political legacy of the division remains in the rivalries perpetuated by the residents of the "Northern" and "Southern" ends of the state today.

The border notwithstanding, New Brunswick was decidedly East Jersey. A short distance from the English colonial capital in Perth Amboy, the first colonists' lives here were defined by hardship, harsh reality and the grinding work necessary to establish permanent settlements. Yet there was also a seemingly boundless freedom to determine one's fate.

Many of the difficulties in settling the early colonial wilderness were offset by the widely available natural resources within it. Of course, it was that very same wilderness that terrified people in their day-to-day lives. Creeping through marshy wetlands into deep, dark woods where a foreboding quiet loomed over the settlers was an everyday occurrence. It's no wonder people were in a hurry to tame the landscape!

Still, development was slow. Many who passed through the area went on to look for opportunities elsewhere, but some who arrived did see potential. Daniel Cooper, the earliest known settler, established a ferry to cross the Raritan River near modern-day Albany Street.

Later, John Inian and a group of ten investors purchased huge tracts of land from the natives. They carved out lots of varying acreage, divided up their property boundaries and worked to sell titles to new settlers. John Prigmore was one early developer whose swampy parcels would one day become New Brunswick as we know it.

The semblance of an established order was just coming into existence throughout the North American colonies. However, early jurisprudence in the 1600s was counterweighted to some degree by an element of lawlessness.

European settlers understood that the only rules that actually existed were the ones they collectively agreed on in practice. A bad actor could easily circumvent or even thwart the law. Roguish behavior was not uncommon. Pirates openly roamed and faced little resistance.

Not cooperating with the pirates could be costly. These villains were likely to loot, plunder and burn down the property of perceived enemies. On the contrary, working with pirates was often beneficial, even profitable. A number of early American families' wealth was derived from doing business with pirates, investing in their expeditions and fencing their plundered goods.

Pirates operated within a network of powerful associates and could leverage their connections for favors. Bribing politicians to allow pirates free movement throughout the colonies was not unusual. Without the protection or fear of the law in place, there was plenty of tacit and even outright support for piracy among colonists.

It wasn't a difficult choice for many to make and in many ways, the presence of pirates was welcomed. This so-called Golden Age of Piracy lasted roughly eighty years, from 1650 to 1730.

HAUNTED TREASURE

Of course, with stories of pirates come rumors of treasure. In some cases, there are whispers of *haunted* treasure no less. In 1729, toward the end of the great pirate epoch, a young Patriot named Benjamin Franklin described a curious phenomenon he'd observed after spending time in New Jersey on a government contract printing colonial currency.

Franklin wrote how large numbers of people were convinced that undiscovered treasure hoards buried by pirates were simply waiting to be unearthed. He described how men would wander by day through the bushes and woods divining secret marks and signs on the trees. They would return at midnight (the appointed hour for such expeditions) to dig for buried gold.

With every thrust of their shovels, they'd hope to strike riches yet tremble with fear at the possibility that they would encounter the malicious demons known to be guarding the wealth. When the hole they created was ultimately found to be lacking, the superstitious treasure hunters reasoned that some force had somehow pushed the cache farther down, just beyond the tips of their pickaxes, never doubting their insights or ability to correctly identify a spot marked for buried treasure.

The famously pragmatic Franklin dismissed the entire practice as foolish. Wealth was found in industry and frugality, he argued—not at the end of a spade. Yet he also noted that the practice of searching for pirate treasure was so common that one could hardly walk half a mile out of town without observing several pits dug for that very purpose.

Was the hunt for gold as silly as Franklin made it out to be? The lonesome and secluded shores of New Jersey's rivers and tributaries would have made a convenient locale for stashing or hiding loot. Regular visits to New Jersey by some of the most infamous scallywags to roam the seas during this era are well known.

Captain Kidd overseeing the burial of his treasure. *Public domain image by Howard Pyle, from the Library of Congress.*

Portrait of
Benjamin Franklin.
*Public domain image
by Charles Wilson
Peale, from the Library
of Congress.*

Captain Morgan is believed to have reached our shores. Legend has it that Howell Davis—an Odysseus-like pirate known for his cunning and trickery—married a Jersey girl. Edward Teach, more commonly known as the fearsome Blackbeard, sailed up the Delaware River. Each is rumored to have buried a stash of gold and jewels somewhere around the Garden State.

Unlike these legends of dubious origin, however, Captain Kidd is *known* to have docked in the Raritan Bay shortly after his greatest adventure. In 1697, the plunder of a wealthy Indian ship secured his status as a rich man. It likewise sealed his fate as a hated pirate. Of course, he, too, is suspected of hiding his treasure nearby.

While heading north to Boston from the Caribbean, Kidd docked at the mouth of the Raritan River. His purpose? Using his newfound riches to bribe crooked politicians and officials in the area for protection.

Reports suggest that he buried significant portions of the money throughout New Jersey and neighboring New York. Kidd's stockpile of gold and gems is rumored to be worth millions of dollars today. Despite bits and pieces washing ashore now and again, the motherlode has never been found.

A Secret Code

The Raritan River empties into the Raritan Bay, where Captain Kidd was anchored. It is conceivable and even plausible that he traveled up the river to New Brunswick on that fateful excursion. A local mystery suggests that his treasure may have been found locally at some point, only to be lost again.

According to the life's work of local historian and researcher Ann Alvarez, the two teenagers Elias Suydam and Henry Monroe Danbury were neighbors and friends from New Brunswick. In 1876, these young men charted a course downstream together along the Raritan River and its tributaries. Along their route, they carved mysterious messages into large rocks with professional precision. Incredibly, their engravings seem to imply or suggest the knowledge of a buried treasure.

Employing the use of strange symbols, obscure references and secret codes on at least five separate sites, each within a four-mile radius of one another, they dangled clues for posterity about a secret they possessed. If there were more messages, they have not yet been found or have been destroyed. The surviving sites are all marked with these young men's names or initials, as well as hints that appear designed to lead the viewer someplace.

For instance, at one site, they carved crude nautical coordinates: S95W4. One common form of nautical measurement is a "chain," or the equivalent of a tenth of a nautical mile. Go roughly southwest almost ten chains from that spot and it leads to a small path and another set of carvings downstream—an intentional trail.

Several of the stones also depict open treasure chests, and almost all of their stones are marked with a signature skull and crossbones. In a clear reference to pirates, some of the boys' skulls are depicted wearing a patch over one eye.

Stranger still, it appears that Danbury and Suydam somehow gained access to a set of secret, high order Masonic symbols and used these tools to convey some of their hidden messages. Their most elaborate carving is a

A mysterious skull carving on the rocks along the Lawrence Brook. *Photo by Mark Moran, courtesy of ©WeirdNJ.com.*

The hidden message may reveal the words "Red Rover." *Photo by Mark Moran, courtesy of ©WeirdNJ.com.*

Masonic cryptogram—a set of symbols that depict an encrypted code with occult significance.

The unique symbols that were diligently chiseled into the limestone appear beneath the beautifully wrought phrase "Centennial Year." The strangely decorated boulder, which can still be found today on a lonely trail beside Lawrence Brook, has been dubbed Centennial Rock.

The Freemasons are a mysterious and powerful group infamously responsible for keeping the secrets of their organization. Julie Tibbott, author of the book *Members Only: Secret Societies, Sects, and Cults Exposed!*, writes that Freemasonry is best understood as "a system of morality, veiled in allegory, illustrated by signs and symbols."

Within the Freemason fraternal order is a hierarchical status referred to by a system of degrees. Tibbott explains that "Masonic ritual is centered around the ascension through these degrees," with the third and highest step being Master Mason. Achieving this status entails correctly answering questions utilizing the memorization of many facts, thus the phrase to give someone "the third degree."

Becoming a Master Mason enables a member to join appendant Masonic lodges, which confer additional degrees. The Royal Arch Degree is one such affiliation. Important symbols associated with the Royal Arch Degree include a keystone, a pentagram within a circle and stone arches. It is exactly these symbols that Suydam and Danbury used in their carvings.

The use of the symbology of this degree in itself may be a reference to secret treasure. The construction of the biblical King Solomon's temple in Jerusalem is the inspiration for a number of Masonic legends and traditions. The Legend of Enoch is one specifically associated with the Royal Arch Degree. The allegory describes in some detail how a fortune of vast wealth and knowledge was buried beneath King Solomon's temple.

According to the legend, Enoch was granted a vision of heavenly inspiration and voluminous knowledge of the world, the sun, the moon and the stars. He constructed a deep vault on Mount Moriah to house a triangular plate of gold encrusted with jewels and inscribed with his knowledge. This was the spot where Solomon would one day build his temple.

Historically, the signs and symbols used by the Freemasons were closely guarded private references for use by society members, but today, many have been revealed. Anyone with the inclination to do a little investigation online can learn many of their so-called secrets.

At the time when Danbury and Suydam were using these same secrets to communicate in 1876, however, the information was much harder to come by. Given their youth, it is unlikely that they were high-ranking Masons. It is surprising then to see the number of references they used which were ostensibly off limits. It appears that Danbury and Suydam had somehow stumbled on knowledge that was not meant for them.

The Royal Arch Masons traded their secret messages using a cipher, a method used to encode information. Suydam and Danbury's intricate 1876 stone carving appears to use this very code. Cryptologists who have reviewed the carvings on Centennial Rock recognize the strange markings as derivative of the Royal Arch cipher. Ann Alvarez's research suggests that the inscription likely spells the coded message "RED ROVER." Importantly, Suydam and Danbury also carved the same words "RED ROVER" elsewhere, without encryption.

THE RED ROVER CONNECTION

The use of Masonic symbols and other hidden references are an indicator that Suydam and Danbury possessed valuable information with a possible connection to buried treasure. The significance of these cryptic messages may lie in the revenants of the earliest days of colonial America, the revolutionary birth of the United States and the emergence of American democracy.

Red Rover was the name of an actual pirate and Scottish privateer who operated in the fourteenth century, but this is probably not the reference Suydam and Danbury were making. Instead, it is more plausible that they were suggesting a connection to *The Red Rover*, a popular 1827 novel by famous American author (and New Jersey native) James Fenimore Cooper.

Cooper's contributions to early American literature often depicted Indigenous and colonial characters. *The Red Rover* tells the story of three sailors who encounter the fearsome titular pirate. Along with all the adventure and maritime escapades one expects in a great seafaring novel, the main characters fight a naval battle to the death over Red Rover's treasure.

While Cooper's *Red Rover* is a rousing piece of fiction, like all great stories, there is an element of truth buried within it. In 1949, literary scholar Willard Hallam Bonner made the case that anyone familiar with the legend of Captain Kidd could easily make the connection that the character "Red Rover" is an obvious stand-in for the real-life historical pirate.

Portrait of the author of *The Red Rover*, New Jersey native James Fenimore Cooper. *Public domain image, from the New York Public Library Digital Collections.*

Is that the reference Danbury and Suydam made, too? Perhaps the secret of the mysterious rocks of New Brunswick reveals a treasure map to Kidd's treasure for whoever can unlock their final meaning. In any case, the repeated use of the "RED ROVER" reference must reveal something significant about the solution.

There is at least one more interpretation of the reference though. Bonner also points out that James Fenimore Cooper may be regarded as a fervid American Patriot who became a novelist by accident. The subtext of many of his stories was that American democracy was a fragile yet profound experiment. His books were often vehicles for thinly veiled democratic propaganda.

While Captain Kidd is the obvious reference for the Red Rover, Suydam and Danbury may have shared a more nuanced interpretation of the so-called villain, one tied to the patriotic fervor of the nation's centennial celebrations in which the boys were no doubt swept up. Bonner wrote, "Cooper consciously cuts himself loose from the legends of Captain Kidd to present a roving patriot in the period of calm that preceded the storm of the Revolution."

He further explained that Cooper "caught the early spirit of independence that disregarded English law, that in the Revolution was patriotic and good, but that before that time had been criminal." In other words, the Red Rover may be the symbol for a Patriot who was regarded as a pirate.

During the Revolutionary War, New Brunswick was a hotbed of activity on both sides of the conflict. The British occupied the city for six months during the winter from 1776 to 1777, and their capacity to resupply their troops rested on the ability to access the port at New Brunswick.

Unfortunately for them, the cliffs along the winding bends of the Raritan River provided ample opportunity for hidden American cannons to disrupt British movement. After a string of stinging defeats for the Continental army, Alexander Hamilton even positioned a battery of artillery there to guard Washington's retreat across New Jersey. Hamilton's cannons delayed the British pursuit long enough for the tidal laps of the Raritan to cover the ford necessary to cross the water.

Not only did the British have to worry about well-placed cannons, but American privateers who profited from the plunder and destruction of British vessels were also a real hindrance to the British movement of goods and their ability to prosecute the war. In New Brunswick, a vital logistical node for the British, the threat of a disrupted merchant supply chain was more than enough to seriously concern the British commanders.

Local hero Adam Hyler was one such pest for the British. This Patriot privateer lived in New Brunswick, and his prowess at commandeering enemy ships became the fodder for legends. Operating in secret directly under the noses of British officials and military command, Hyler conducted lightning-fast raids using lightly armed whaleboats to seize merchant ships, capture their crews, plunder the goods on board and finally burn the vessels.

Between 1778 and 1782, Hyler relentlessly harassed the British fleet. One story recounts how Hyler led a small armada of sloops from the prow of the good ship *Revenge*. He captured five British ships in one night, looted the cargo from four of them and then burned them. He left the fifth intact due to it having women and children on board.

The tale demonstrates that despite his fervent support for the cause of independence, he was not a murderous pirate. Regardless, Hyler's maneuvers undoubtedly allowed him to accumulate enormous personal gains at the British expense.

In his time as a privateer between 1780 and 1782, Hyler burned or captured more than thirty boats. He accumulated enough stores and goods to sustain forty men for four months, as well as valuable assets like cash, silver spoons and candlesticks. He also kidnapped and ransomed fifty or so prisoners, including high-ranking officers like General Jacob S. Jackson, Captains John White and James Corlies and a Hessian major.

When Hyler died in August 1782, it was under mysterious circumstances. Some accounts suggest that he was poisoned in a tavern. Others say that he died from complications after taking a bullet to the leg. Some suggest that it was he who literally shot himself in the foot!

It's presumed that after selling his acquisitions and splitting the loot with his men, Hyler's share would have been considerable. It doesn't seem likely that he was able to spend his fortune before he perished. He did have a will, which was faithfully executed, but after his death, his wife complained in court that she was not provided enough to live on.

How could such a wealthy man's widow go without? The mystery concerning the whereabouts of his assets has never been answered.

Mysteries Remain

A hidden cache of treasure somewhere in the vicinity of New Brunswick is an intriguing and tantalizing possibility. A number of caves, tunnels and mines that might have served as hiding places are contained in the historical record.

Unfortunately, there are more questions than answers when it comes to solving the mysteries of the Danbury and Suydam carvings. Their trail of

Revolutionary privateer Captain Hyler barking orders to his crew. *Public domain image by James Otis, from the Library of Congress.*

clues may have been an elaborate prank, but this does not account for their knowledge of Masonic secrets. Neither does it dismiss the fact that Captain Kidd's treasure remains lost, nor the notion that the whereabouts of Adam Hyler's fortune is unknown.

When it comes to New Brunswick's pirates and privateers, there is perhaps more "story" than history recounted in the legends. Until the puzzles that were left for us in the rocks are unlocked, however, the answers will continue to remain elusive.

THE GHOSTS
OF BUCCLEUCH MANSION

Buccleuch Mansion looms high on a hill overlooking the Raritan River. The imposing Georgian colonial home is an anachronistic structure. Standing out among the modern picnic pavilions and soccer fields dotting Buccleuch Park (pronounced "buck-lew"), the house endures as a fixed reminder of New Brunswick's distant past.

Maintenance of the building over the centuries has been performed in fits and starts as ownership and responsibility for the home changed hands over time. While its upkeep has sometimes languished and its former glory has almost faded, the majesty of the structure remains apparent beneath the cosmetic defects of superficial wear and tear.

The house, as they say, has good bones. Buccleuch has stood since the earliest days of English settlement in New Brunswick. It is a symbol of endurance despite the periods of turbulent division and dissent it has survived. As the oldest remaining building within the city limits, there is considerable history here, and stories of hauntings persist. A fantastic ghost tale has even been passed down through the ages.

Who (or what) haunts the halls of Buccleuch? Its storied past may reveal such insights.

Buccleuch Mansion looms over the Raritan River. *From the Library of Congress.*

A HAUNTED HOUSE

It is popular belief that ghosts are the spirits of the dead. They remain tethered to the mortal world for some inexplicable reason, perhaps if only to scare the pants off unsuspecting victims. However, professional paranormal investigators suggest that while interactive spirits like these may indeed exist, they are exceedingly rare. Such "ghost hunters" have observed and documented a more common yet no less strange phenomenon.

Eric Mintel is the leader of one such paranormal investigation team. According to Mintel, a "ghost" is more often than not the residue of some previous outburst of strong feeling or surge of passionate emotion. Somehow, that flash of energy made an invisible imprint on its surrounding environment. When the remnants of this stored energy are finally released, it manifests in different ways. Some describe it as a prior event being recorded, getting caught in a loop and then playing on repeat until it can be observed.

Sensitive equipment can be used to capture otherwise inaudible sounds and drastic local changes in temperature. Sometimes the energy even becomes visible or otherwise observable to people through noises or smells. Common occurrences include the sounds of inexplicable footsteps overhead, doors slamming and even apparitions. Those who experience this kind of activity are likely to describe the event as a ghost.

Family strife and generational dissent might yield the type of energy required to make a ghostly imprint on the environment. In such a case, Buccleuch is a good contender for the kind of energy that yields a haunting.

THE WHITE FAMILY FARM

In the years leading up to the first sale of the estate in 1774, revolutionary ideals were sweeping the fledgling nation. Impassioned speeches, violent arguments and fiery rhetoric fueled the divisions that split the country. Families sometimes ruptured along the same lines. The first owners of Buccleuch witnessed the overthrow and dissolution of the colonial system and likewise experienced its effects within their own family.

The mansion itself was constructed between 1735 and 1739 by Colonel Anthony White III, a wealthy Englishman. He built the home for his bride, Elizabeth Morris, the daughter of Lewis Morris, the royal governor of New York and New Jersey. Elizabeth's and Anthony's marriage represented a union of political power and the wealth generated by the English colonial system. The homestead established a foundation for their family.

Originally named the White House, the estate included a working farm and a formal garden, which reflected the social status of the family. In time, the Whites raised four children there: Isabella, Johanna, Euphemia and their only son, Anthony Walton.

In the years that followed, Elizabeth and Anthony would maintain allegiance to the Crown and the colonial system that had allowed their family to prosper. However, the heady ideals of independence were awakened in the next generation.

Despite their parents' traditional loyalty, three of the four White children were either directly involved with the Revolution or else became intimately connected with some of its most famous participants.

FAMILY REVOLUTIONS

The youngest, Anthony Walton White, was a fervent Patriot who directly served General George Washington as an aide-de-camp, a secretarial assistant position. He later became an officer and fought in the Battle of Monmouth, but he saw action as far away from home as Georgia and South Carolina. His remains were buried at New Brunswick's Christ Church Episcopal Churchyard, where he is noted as a veteran of the Revolutionary War.

In 1784, Euphemia White married William Paterson, and the couple moved together to New Brunswick. Although he never saw active service, Paterson was a founding father who had been involved in a number of capacities during the Revolutionary War. He most prominently served as attorney general, prosecuting Loyalists and helping maintain order during the turbulent period from 1776 to the end of the war in 1783.

Paterson later served as a justice on the Supreme Court, as well as the second governor of New Jersey. He traveled extensively in his multiple capacities and would often write to Euphemia. In his letters, he expressed affection for her and gratitude for always treating his children from a previous marriage with tender care. Paterson died in 1806, but Euphemia lived comfortably afterward for another twenty-six years. She is buried at the graveyard of the First Presbyterian Church in New Brunswick.

Her sister Johanna White was a third wife to John Bayard. They were married in 1787 and relocated in 1788 to New Brunswick, where Bayard was elected mayor in 1790. He, too, was actively involved in the Revolution. He first supplied arms to the Continental Congress in 1776 and then served as a colonel to a volunteer regiment out of Philadelphia, fighting in the Battles of Brandywine, Germantown and Princeton.

Bayard died in 1807. Johanna survived him by another twenty-four years. In her later life, Johanna resided near her sister Euphemia in Franklin, the town bordering New Brunswick. She is buried near her sister at First Presbyterian Church in New Brunswick.

Isabella, the eldest daughter of the Whites, died unmarried and relatively young in 1789 shortly after their father, only a few years after their mother in 1784. When she died, she left her sister Euphemia a "wench" (a term for a Black servant girl, likely a slave in this instance), her niece Cornelia Paterson a silver coffeepot and her brother-in-law William Paterson $100 plus a lot in New York to be shared with her sister Johanna.

Above, left: Portrait of Brigadier General Anthony Walton White, the young man who grew up in the White House mansion and went on to serve George Washington. *Public domain image by Anna M.W. Woodhull, from the Library of Congress.*

Above, right: Portrait of Euphemia White's husband, William Paterson. *Public domain image, from the New York Public Library Digital Collections.*

Left: Portrait of Johanna White's husband, Colonel John Bayard. *Public domain image, from the New York Public Library Digital Collections.*

In the years leading up to the Revolution, the imprints left by the family in their childhood home that found itself divided along political lines can only be imagined. Perhaps it was the generational gulfs and chasms that led to the sale of the house just before the outbreak of the war. What conversations, what arguments, what passions lingered in its halls?

THE TIDES OF WAR

The family members raised at the White House Farm leveraged their wealth and influence into political power as governance switched from the colonial system to the ideals of the republic. The house itself would also become emblematic of endurance despite the changing tides of the war.

After the Whites left the property, possession of the farm passed back and forth between Loyalists and Patriots during the Revolutionary War. In 1774, the home was purchased by General William Burton. He and his recently married wife, Isabella Auchmuty, lived there until the start of the war.

At that point, Loyalist property was confiscated by New Jersey's revolutionary transitional government. The Commission of Forfeited Estates took ownership of the farm in 1776 through the end of the war.

However, direct control over the estate and the occupants of the house continued to vacillate with the changing ebbs and flows of the conflict. In 1776, Captain George Janeway of New York and his family occupied the

Portrait of White Mansion guest Thaddeus Kosciuszko taking it easy. *Public domain image, from the New York Public Library Digital Collections.*

mansion in New Brunswick when they were compelled to leave Manhattan after the British took control of the city.

During this time, founding fathers George Washington and Alexander Hamilton were visitors to the house. Other notable Revolutionary War figures who stayed there include Horatio Gates, a controversial commander who once attempted to oust Washington as general, and Thaddeus Kosciuszko, a Polish freedom fighter and military engineer who designed successful fortifications for the Americans during the war.

By 1777, however, the British were occupying New Brunswick, and control of the property fell into the hands of the British once again. Officers of the Ennis Killen Dragoons quartered in the mansion.

Maintenance of the house (or the lack of it) was entrusted to these transitory residents; damage to the original floorboards where guns and sabers were stacked on the third story is still evident in the house today.

A RESIDENT GHOST

After the war, the White Farm estate was put up for sale and purchased by a number of people over the next several decades. By 1821, a prominent lawyer named Colonel Joseph Warren Scott had purchased the house. Scott renamed the house Buccleuch in honor of his Scottish ancestry, and it was during his tenure as the owner when the most well-known ghost story associated with the house was publicized.

In 1842, "An Evening at Buccleuch Hall" was published in the *Ladies' Companion*, a monthly magazine devoted to literature and the fine arts. The story was quickly republished as "The Grenadier's Ghost; a Tale of the Old Stair Head Clock" in newspapers around the country. Such tantalizing ghost stories were popular fodder for audiences during the Victorian era.

The author, Joseph Holt Ingraham, related a story he heard one dark and stormy night while he and a party of travelers passing through New Brunswick stayed in the "ancient manor." In his telling, Colonel Scott showed his guests through the house and described its tumultuous history.

Ingraham wrote, "Every sword hack on the black oaken banister, every indent of a musket muzzle on the broad stairs, every gouge in the wainscot made by a bayonet, [was] sacred in his eyes."

With lightning and thunder crashing, the talk soon turned to ghosts. Scott revealed that he indeed has been visited by the dead one night a few years before, on a night just like the one outside. The guests clamored for the tale, and he imparted the following story.

On a blustery October night about a decade prior to their visit, Colonel Scott was alone in his house, aside from a lone servant named Harry who had already retired to bed. Scott was in his study poring over texts by candlelight when he was surprised to hear the old grandfather clock at the top of the staircase outside his library strike midnight.

Wondering how it had gotten to be so late, the colonel poured himself a glass of port wine to quiet his thoughts before falling asleep. Reposed in silent reflection and contemplation with the snifter in hand ("a rare old brand few cellars in the Jersies could furnish"), he became concerned by the noise of heavy footsteps descending the steps outside his study.

When the stamp of the footfall reached the landing, the house "trembled" and the wine "tremulated" in its glass. Scott was overcome by an acute sensation of fear and the dread of "otherworldly intuition." He pulled a sword from its scabbard on the wall and readied himself as the "military tred" and the "jangling of arms" slowly approached the other side of the entrance.

All at once, Scott thrust open the door to the room. There he was, face to face with a decomposing skeleton dressed in the moldy uniform of a captain of a British grenadier, a regiment of the royal infantry. The monster carried a lantern flickering with a dying light.

Stunned, Colonel Scott stood aside as the living corpse staggered its way into the room. It approached a small shelf on which a variety of odds and ends were stored. The grenadier filled his lantern with a can of oil that rested there and appeared to smile with some satisfaction.

Scott asked the ghost what he would have next, whereupon the ghost "replied in a deep sepulchral voice, 'Wine.'" Scott implored it to help itself, and the story changed tone, becoming humorous. The two proceed to toast each other, drink most of the bottle of port and smoke a pair of the colonel's good cigars together.

The satisfied ghost promised to reveal a secret mystery related to "the cause of [his] nightly wanderings" and "the treasure of the old White family, which they concealed on the premises when they deserted the mansion." But first, he said, "Let us have another glass…to wash the cobwebs down that have been choking up my cogs these seventy years, and then I will begin."

With that, however, the clock struck one and marked the passage of an hour. The chimes sounded much louder and closer to Scott than usual.

What mysteries still linger in the halls of Buccleuch Mansion? The haunted clock remains standing in the hall as a relic of a bygone era. *From the Library of Congress.*

Before it could reveal the whereabouts of the treasure, the ghost announced its departure.

It ascended the steps to the landing, where the clock usually stood, followed by Scott. As they approached the top of the stairs together, the ghost assumed a place beside the wall and finally transformed into the clock.

Despite its promise to return, Scott informed his guests that the ghost was never seen again. The article finally reports that while none in attendance believed the tale, the fear of the group was palpable.

TRUE MYSTERIES

This fantastic story was passed down through oral tradition and was periodically reported by local media outlets. A contributing writer to a 1932 *Home News Tribune* article that reprinted the story establishes the significance of Ingraham's literary body of work. A 1979 article from the same paper debates the merits of the story's claims.

According to an expert in that article, folklore passed down by Brunswick locals argued that "a tunnel was constructed during Revolutionary times

Left: The partially exposed tunnel uncovered during the expansion of Route 18, subsequently destroyed. *Photo by Ann Alvarez.*

Below: An engraved stone recovered from the lost tunnel extending below Buccleuch Mansion. *Photo by Mark Neurohr-Pierpaoli.*

from the White House cellar down the hill to the Raritan. Supposedly, the tunnel was used to smuggle arms and supplies by the rebels from silent barges on the river. Others believe the tunnel was made as an escape route for fleeing rebels." At that time, however, the house did not appear to have any such secret passages.

And yet just the very thing was discovered a few years after the 1979 article. The storied tunnel was, in fact, uncovered on the Buccleuch property during the construction phase of the Route 18 widening project. It was apparently not always a secret though. A number of visitors over the years were found to have carved their names on its stone walls (including the notorious stone carvers from the previous chapter).

Sadly, no one will ever know if this is the place where New Brunswick's long-purported treasure was ever hidden. The entrance to the tunnel was destroyed within a few days to advance the construction of Route 18. Recognizing the potential importance of the engravings, though, several stones were excavated and preserved before the tunnel was lost.

Today, the Daughters of the American Revolution maintain these stones on the Buccleuch property in an outdoor garden open to the public. They are also responsible for maintaining the interior of the house, where, in fact, the famous clock from the story is still standing in the halls of Buccleuch Mansion.

The City of New Brunswick maintains responsibility for the outside and its environs. The house is open to the public, but visiting hours are infrequent and sporadic. It's best to contact the DAR to schedule a tour.

For now, Buccleuch Manor rests silently, still visible from the very highway whose construction unearthed a part of its story. As always, the quiet house on the hill endures as a fixed reminder of New Brunswick's distant past.

MIDWIVES AND MONSTERS

F olklore consists of telling the same stories over and over again, sometimes for centuries or millennia. It may be that this ancient tradition helped early people to manage the unpredictable elements of the wild, allowing humans to thrive. Today, such stories brought by older generations to a new location help orient in new environments by recalling a familiar setting.

New Brunswick has enjoyed waves of immigrants from different countries over many decades. Starting in the mid-nineteenth century, New Brunswick was home to a large population of Hungarian immigrants that began to significantly increase in the 1880s. Immigration continued to increase through the 1920s and first peaked in the early twentieth century. By 1949, one estimate placed the Hungarian community in New Brunswick at twelve to thirteen thousand people, or roughly one-third of the city's population at the time.

These first- and second-generation Hungarian Americans were spread over multiple city wards but were predominantly centered in the triangle of space bounded by Easton Avenue, French Street and the Mile Run Brook at the western edge of the city. The area was commonly known as "Little Hungary."

Packed into a neighborhood where at any time the aromas of paprika and sizzling onions wafted down the street, the sheer number of Hungarians was large enough to support two weekly local Hungarian-language newspapers. It was not uncommon to see "Magyar Ustet" ("Hungarian Spoken") on

Vestiges of Little Hungary remain standing beside major modern developments in the old neighborhood. *Photo by Mark Neurohr-Pierpaoli.*

store windows throughout the city, especially along French Street, the main Hungarian economic corridor at the time.

As the first rounds of immigrants from Hungary assimilated to life in America, the wave of newly arrived Hungarians to New Brunswick continued to swell. Thousands fleeing from the Hungarian Revolution of 1956 joined the Hungarian community already established in New Brunswick, which would soon be referred to as the most Hungarian city in the United States.

At the height of their resettlement here, Hungarians built on the foundations laid by previous generations and contributed to the cultural, civic, religious and economic vitality of New Brunswick.

Today, although the number of Hungarians living within city limits has dwindled, vestiges of their history remain. The City of New Brunswick even maintains diplomatic ties with Debrecen, an official sister city and the capital of Hungary's Northern Great Plain region.

The first statue of the hero Cardinal Mindszenty, a stalwart opponent of Stalinism. *Photo by Mark Neurohr-Pierpaoli.*

A monument to the victims of the Hungarian uprising crushed by the Soviet Union in 1956. *Photo by Mark Neurohr-Pierpaoli.*

In New Brunswick, at the corner of Somerset and Plum Streets, a statue of Hungarian cardinal József Mindszenty, staunch opponent of Stalinism, stands across from a monument to the victims of the 1956 Hungarian Revolution.

Religious services are still held at the historic Saint Ladislaus Church, once the beating heart of the Hungarian community. The congregation has since merged with other churches and now goes by the name Holy Family Parish.

A relief portrait of St. Ladislaus on the exterior of the namesake church. *Photo by Mark Neurohr-Pierpaoli.*

The nearby Hungarian Scouts headquarters maintains a link between older generations and Hungarian American youth. The Hungarian American Athletic Club, first established in 1913, remains a fixture of the community as a hub for programs like dinner dances and cultural events, as well as a headquarters for Hungarian cultural organizations.

The American Hungarian Foundation operates the Hungarian Heritage Center on Somerset Street to maintain its archives, a museum and its

The annual festival celebrates Hungarian culture and folklife on the first Saturday in June. *Photo by Mark Neurohr-Pierpaoli.*

library as an affiliate of the Rutgers library. It also hosts the popular annual Hungarian festival, held on the first Saturday of June every summer. This event sees the return of thousands of the far-flung descendants of the first inhabitants of Little Hungary. The streets of New Brunswick are filled with locals and visitors alike to celebrate Hungarian culture through traditional food, folk songs and dances.

FAMILIAR FOLKLORE

Hungarian culture continues to be passed down from one generation to the next. Hungarians have always engaged in a rich tradition of telling folktales involving mythological figures and people with supernatural powers. Many of these stories continued to be told until the second half of the twentieth century, when the modes of traditional storytelling began to change. Now hardly any of these mythological figures survive. However, at least one creature still remains in popular folklore derived from ancient beliefs: the witch.

According to Csenge Zalka, author of the book *Dancing on Blades: Rare and Exquisite Folktales from the Carpathian Mountains*, the iron-nosed witch (*vasorrú bába*) is a highly recognizable character from Hungarian folktales. She is an old woman with great powers, and her most prominent feature is the metal spike poking from her face right where her nose belongs. She is also sometimes depicted with a set of iron teeth.

Unlike some witches in Hungarian folklore, the *bába* is not merely a mortal woman with powers, but rather an entirely supernatural being. She can bewitch others and change shape. However, tradition states that nobody can become a bába before she has bedeviled someone else. She might learn her witchcraft through a horrific sacrifice, like murdering a child, or else she may learn the profession from her mother.

Zalka relates a story called "The Daughter of the Iron-Nosed Witch." In this tale, the old hag with the pointy metal nose is also, somehow, the mother of a kind and beautiful daughter. The witch mostly keeps the girl locked in the house they share, but every so often the reclusive beauty finds occasion to step outside. Inevitably, the men who encounter her become enamored.

One day, a passing prince and his huntsmen hear the girl singing inside the nearby house. The servants peek in the window to see who has such a lovely voice, and they become frozen in place. The witch, returning from her travels, finds the prince and places a hex on him to also fix him to the spot where he stands, tightly binding "his sinews with a spell."

That night, the girl leaves the house while the witch sleeps to gaze at her reflection in a bottomless pond. She finds the servants and kindly frees them with the brush of a broom before heading to the water.

The loyal men return to their prince only to find him in a similar predicament to their previous state and realize that something strange is happening. They resolve to free the prince and destroy the house of the witch. The servants leave to get help, while the prince remains stuck in place, gazing with longing at the bába's daughter.

The next day, the servants return with horses and strong men to try and drag the prince away, but he cries out in pain as they try to pull him from his spot. He cannot be moved. Hearing the ruckus, the witch comes outside to laugh at the fiasco. The girl closely follows her mother and asks, "How can you do this, mother? Do you wish to kill him like all the others?"

With a wave of her hand and a cruel cackle, the witch dismisses the complaints of her naive daughter and goes back inside. Seeing their opportunity, with the

The iron-nosed witch is a well-known figure in Hungarian folklore. *Public domain image by Andrew Lang and H.J. Ford, via Wikimedia Commons.*

daughter outside and the bába within, the strong men pick up the entire house with the witch inside. They toss the whole thing into the pond. Thus, "the house with the iron-nosed witch sank away from sight like a stone."

In the end, the prince is freed at the touch of the daughter. Of course, the two fall in love after their shared ordeal. Delighted in their newfound freedom, they marry and live together happily ever after.

The relationship between witches and children is a common trope in Hungarian folklore. In a separate tale, a young king marries a woman who promises him two children with golden hair. She fulfills her promise and gives birth to two beautiful blonde boys, but a jealous witch with iron teeth steals the infants from their crib and replaces them with dogs.

The witch buries the children in secret. Horrified that his wife has somehow given birth to the animals, the king demands the "children" and his wife be tossed into the sea. There, a whale swallows the poor woman whole. Through trickery and deceit, the iron-toothed witch soon convinces the king to marry her own daughter instead.

In the ensuing years, the meddling witch and her daughter attempt to hide their crimes, but the truth is magically persistent. A pair of trees grow where the boys were buried. The witch has them cut down. A few beds are made from the wood, but after learning that the beds can speak, the witch has them burned. A passing goat eats some surviving wood from the pile of ashes and gives birth to two golden kids. The witch has the magic goats killed and prepared into a stew. As the goat meat is prepared and cleaned in the river, two pieces break off and turn into goldfish. The fish grow big until they are finally caught by a fisherman one day.

Back on land, the fish transform into the long-buried princes. The humble fisherman brings the boys to the king. There, despite the incessant interruptions of the witch, the two young men are able to reveal the truth. They are the long-lost children of the king, and their mother is still alive in the belly of the whale.

To verify the authenticity of the story, the whale is caught. Sure enough, their mother is freed from its belly, and the king finally believes the truth.

The king asks his council for advice on the punishment the witch and her daughter deserve. In the end, the two are drawn and quartered—dragged through the streets tied to the tail of a horse, cut in four pieces and then hammered with nails into each corner of the kingdom.

Somehow, the surviving family is able to put the horror of their past behind them and live together in happiness and prosperity from that point forward.

THE WITCHES OF NEW BRUNSWICK

While these iron-clad witches of folklore are the stuff of legends and folklore, belief in witchcraft and evil magic was nevertheless a part of day-to-day life among real-life Hungarians.

The Hungarian word *bába* is the same for both a witch and a midwife. A midwife is, of course, a person, usually a woman, who assists other women before, during and after childbirth. Midwifery is a long-standing and noble profession.

One notable example was Magdalene Kovacs, a New Brunswick midwife who primarily served the Hungarian community in the 1920s. She is named among the birth records for assisting in nearly 450 deliveries!

According to beliefs recorded in several parts of Hungary, however, midwives were known to consort with witches. Hungarian records of witch trials frequently mention midwives. This is likely due to the fact that if anything went wrong during childbirth or in the postnatal care of the mother, a midwife was a common scapegoat due to her intimate role in the childbirth process. Indeed, at least one posthumous birth is recorded alongside Kovacs's name, as are several stillbirths.

The sensational 1897 media's depiction of a Hungarian midwife referred to in newspaper headlines as "The Poison Witch" didn't do much to separate the role from its dark associations, either. The *New York World* blasted the news about "a woman who has poisoned more than 100 people" across headlines, describing Azalai Jager Mari as a "Hungarian midwife who practiced murder as a fine art." The yellow journal goes on to describe in grim detail her lurid crimes of infanticide and murder for hire, which led to her conviction and life sentence in Budapest.

Such stories of witchcraft and other occult practices followed Hungarian immigrants to America. Even New Brunswick had a resident witch living on Easton Avenue! In 1915, Julia Horvath gained a reputation for her abilities as a practitioner of the dark arts after she convinced a number of women that she "had the control of evil spirits" and, for a fee, could learn the past, present and future of a person's life, as well as cure diseases.

After collecting more than $80 from one woman over the course of a month (almost $2,500 in today's terms) without delivering on any of her promises, Julia was brought to court on several charges. In her own defense, she stated that she only took a quarter of the alleged sum from the unsuspecting woman. Regardless, she refused to provide a refund.

Tantalizing headlines demonized the "poison witch" midwife from Hungary. *From the* New York World, *July 11, 1897.*

In 1921, *New Brunswick Home News* reported that a similar story had begun to unfold in nearby Milltown. "Professor" Eugene I. Bagonye established an altar on Ryders Lane where he led candle-lit séances to contact the dead in a "weirdly fitted up" parlor with the strangely mixed trappings of "Romanism and demonology."

A New Brunswick woman soon laid charges against the Hungarian spiritualist of "pretending to practice sorcery, conjuration and enchantment," as well as taking five dollars for a powder to do the same. She claimed that she paid the man fifty dollars over several months but became convinced that he was a fake when she was refused a refund.

When she brought the matter to the police, Bagonye denied the accusations of witchcraft or any wrongdoing. He spoke with "intense conviction of his supernatural powers," but he never claimed any ability to tell fortunes or cast horoscopes.

He argued that his séances did not include obvious gimmicks intended to deceive others like table knocking or levitation. He felt that he possessed trancelike psychic and spiritual healing powers. All he claimed he was able to do, though, was to communicate with the spirits of the dead and return their message to his audience. He said that no fee was charged for the séance, and he never took money from anyone except what was freely given to him as a contribution.

While a number of stories like this persisted, not all accusations of witchcraft were associated with scams. Some were motivated by plain old hysteria. In 1936, the *New Brunswick Home News* again followed a story that involved a community of women accusing their neighbor of witchcraft.

Three middle-aged Hungarian women from Woodbridge testified in court before the police recorder that their neighbor was a servant of the devil and a witch, concocting herbal brews and potions to perform acts of black magic and sorcery.

The three produced a litany of wild claims. On different occasions over several years, they said they saw the woman turn herself into a horse and walk on her hind legs, change her own head into a dog's head, swell her body and shrink her head to the size of a fist, grow horns, produce large lumps on her back and shoot blazes of fire from her head. Twenty more women stood ready and waiting in the wings at the courthouse to swear under oath that they had seen the very same with their own eyes.

To no one's surprise, the recipient of the defamation turned the tables on her accusers and pressed charges against them for her public humiliation. The court agreed with the victim and found the first three guilty of disorderly conduct.

Placed on probation for one month, they received instructions not to annoy the woman they accused and to report to the court once a week.

In the following days, Father Lenyi, a local Hungarian priest, sat with the ringleaders, listened to their claims and worked diligently to expose the "absurdity" of their "old-world lore." After many hours of convincing, the primary accusers agreed to abandon their superstitions and promised to live like good neighbors, but the strange beliefs were persistent in the community. Rumors of witches were still being whispered among the terrified townsfolk long after this probation period was finished.

SOME THINGS NEVER CHANGE

A folk tradition of witchcraft was brought to New Brunswick through Hungarian superstition, yet similar folklore is still alive and well in New Brunswick. Nowadays, though, it is from a different part of the world.

As the demographics of the city changed, so did the stories told by new arrivals from foreign places. Today, as in the past, new environments are familiarized through the stories and the beliefs immigrants bring with them.

Throughout the latter half of the twentieth century into the twenty-first, immigrants from Mexico, Central America and the Caribbean have continued to change the population of New Brunswick. The residents of the city now include a Hispanic population over 46 percent.

It's clear that as much as the city grows and changes over time, new light continues to shed new life on the same old stories and traditions, over and over again. Instead of the iron-nosed witches of Hungary, today urban legends about monsters like El Chupacabra or ghosts like La Llorona are brought from the countryside to the streets of New Brunswick.

Similarly, the practices of Afro-Caribbean religions like Santería, Voodoo and Macumba, all of which have drawn so many comparisons to witchcraft, are practiced simply by families in their homes and in small Botanica shops selling candles and potions along French Street.

In a grand tradition dating back more than a century, it's even still possible to obtain a psychic reading on Easton Avenue. Just don't expect any refunds!

RUTGERS RARITIES

I n a college as old as New Brunswick's Rutgers University, first chartered by King George III in 1766, there are bound to be traditions passed down from one class of students to the next throughout the years. Over time, these tall tales take on lives of their own and wind up fueling some pretty weird local legends. Of course, every good yarn has a nugget of truth to it, and the strange, unusual and sometimes spooky stories that are still spread around Rutgers campus are no exception to the rule.

DIFFERENT SCHOOLS OF THOUGHT

For many years, the New Brunswick branch of Rutgers University was divided into distinct and semi-autonomous districts, with each section operating as individual residential colleges under a broad Rutgers umbrella. A university-wide push to consolidate the schools began in 2006, however, and since then, the unification of Rutgers as one university has slowly but surely been taking shape.

With separate admissions and curriculum requirements, each part of the school specialized in different academic subject areas at different times. As a result, each campus has developed its own culture over the years. Some aspects of the divisions linger in a number of ways.

The College Avenue campus of Rutgers remains the historic flagship liberal arts school. College Avenue also happens to be the birthplace of the fat sandwich, a belly-busting loaf of bread stuffed with everything from chicken fingers and mozzarella sticks to gyro meat and cheesesteak.

With names like "Fat Beach" and "Fat Knight," every sandwich is a slight variation on the theme, but they're all traditionally topped with French fries. Served from various mobile "grease trucks" over the years, the popular sandwich is also available at any of the pizza parlors on nearby Easton Avenue after the bars let out.

Students may even have a fat sandwich named in their honor if they consume a certain number in a limited amount of time, but qualifications vary by establishment.

Technically in Piscataway, the Busch campus focuses on natural sciences, engineering and health sciences. Sometimes grouped with Livingston campus via the free Rutgers bus routes required to travel between them, it is known as a suburban-esque campus thanks to its graduate school housing and quiet group living accommodations (think suites instead of dorms).

A candid photograph of the author ordering a fat sandwich in the long-gone grease truck parking lot, circa early 2000s. *From user MJKazin, via Wikimedia Commons.*

It's not always quiet though. On football game days, thousands of students and fans descend on the campus to participate in the carnival-like atmosphere and tailgate parties outside the stadium. Some even stick around to watch the game inside!

Livingston is a modern campus that houses state-of-the-art social science and business schools as well as the Jersey Mike's Arena, a basketball stadium formerly known as the Rutgers Athletic Center (and still lovingly referred to as the RAC). For many years, however, the campus's defining features were underdevelopment and the Brutalist architectural designs of its various residence halls and academic buildings.

One popular myth is the dubious claim that campus buildings like these were designed to prevent rioters from scaling walls during the tumultuous 1960s. It's more likely that these buildings were simply representative of architectural trends of the time. In any event, newer construction like the three-screen movie theater and a retro-themed diner has finally begun to overshadow such older and undeniably uglier buildings.

Similar to the Busch/Livingston dynamic, the distinction between Douglass and Cook campuses is often blurred, usually referred to in the same breath. For many years, though, Douglass was famously known as a separate residential women's college.

Unbelievably, Rutgers College did not first admit women until 1972. Until the whole school became coeducational, if a young woman were to apply to Rutgers, she might be directed to send the paperwork to Douglass College instead.

Passion Puddle is a scenic pond located between Cook and Douglass campuses that is widely recognized as an iconic spot for budding young love. From time to time, a young man from Cook and a young woman from Douglass may be seen holding hands, ambling around its quietly lapping shores as the pink flowering trees bloom around them.

The popular belief is that if a couple makes their around the water three times in such a fashion, they will one day be happily married. While the origin of the legend is uncertain, circling the pond has become a romantic form of marriage proposal and engagement in recent years.

This is strange, though, given the other lesser-known story associated with the pond. Cook campus highlights programs in the agricultural and environmental sciences. According to legend, a right whale once managed to swim partway up the Raritan River and beached itself on the banks before perishing.

View west across Passion Puddle on the Cook/Douglass Campus of Rutgers University. *From user Famartin, via Wikimedia Commons.*

Never ones to let a scientific opportunity slip through their fingers, Cook student scientists somehow managed to drag the carcass to Passion Puddle, where they worked to remove the skeleton and put it on display at the Rutgers Geology museum. As for the rest of the remains? Many attribute the pond's notoriously cloudy water to the belief that most of the whale sank to the bottom in the process and was left there for good.

The whale isn't the only unusual animal at Rutgers. The research farms on Cook maintain herds of livestock, and the most popular cow on campus is Hyacinth. As a fistulated cow, she boasts a port window into one of her four stomachs so students can observe her digestion process. It is even possible to stick an arm inside her to lend a hand!

For those concerned about her welfare, Rutgers scientists insist that she isn't aware of the hole in her side. They go so far to say that she loves the perquisites of the job, namely, all the extra food and plenty of attention. She doesn't even seem to mind people standing around to watch her eat. Hole-y cow!

HISTORY AND TRADITIONS

Rutgers today looks a lot different than it did when it first started. Although it's up for debate whether the third public reading of the Declaration of Independence in July 1776 took place in downtown New Brunswick or in Easton, Pennsylvania (it may come down to a matter of minutes, although tradition states the readings occurred simultaneously at noon), by the time it happened, Queens College had already been established for a decade.

Rutgers University wouldn't adopt its current name until 1825, after a generous gift from its namesake, Henry Rutgers. The forerunner college was a small and somewhat financially unstable institution for a number of years before it found its footing. It didn't even put up its first buildings until 1809.

Up to that point, students would attend their classes in a variety of private spaces. The first scholars at Queens College established a precedent of taking their lectures in downtown taverns. The Sign of the Red Lion, well known for its strong ale and hearty fare, was a favorite spot among the student body.

Although the former locations of colonial taverns like these are now technically located beneath Route 18, the informal yet well-worn tradition of continuing education in New Brunswick's modern downtown bars and pubs is still popular among Rutgers students today.

Old Queens, the oldest building on Rutgers campus, still stands as a testament to its sturdy masonry. It was built on a former apple orchard donated by James Parker Jr., a wealthy area merchant. The cornerstone was laid by Dr. Ira Condict, a beloved pastor of the city's First Reformed Church, whose ceremonial duties that morning were reportedly undeterred by his arm being held in a sling that week.

However, recent research has uncovered and highlighted the efforts of the unpaid workers who contributed to the rest of its construction. When the foundations were laid in 1809, it was with the use of enslaved labor. By 1810, the town had a population of 2,826 free white persons, 52 free African Americans and 164 enslaved people.

Today, the path from Old Queens to Hamilton Street is named Will's Way in honor of one of those men who worked to build Old Queens. According to the Scarlet and Black Digital Archive, "Will was a man enslaved by Jacon Dunham and hired out to Abraham Blauvelt for performing labor on Old Queens foundation," performing strenuous manual work that, until now, went unrecognized.

The formal acknowledgment of Will and the unknown others like him who aided in the building of the school is an attempt to recognize the

Left: A portrait of the college's namesake, Henry Rutgers. *Public domain image, from the New York Public Library Digital Collections.*

Below: A snowy view of the gate at Old Queens and Will's Way. *From user Rickyrab, via Wikimedia Commons.*

Opposite: Kitty Livingston's staid appearance belies her saucy correspondence with Alexander Hamilton. *Public domain image, from the New York Public Library Digital Collections.*

university's connection to slavery. The ways in which educational institutions have benefited from historical slave labor remains an ongoing conversation among colleges and universities throughout the country.

Old Queens itself happens to be one of the more reportedly haunted buildings on the College Avenue campus. Will hasn't made an appearance, but the ghostly figure of a "gray lady" has been seen here time and time again. Her story lends itself to a haunting legend steeped in history.

Alexander Hamilton, one of America's founding fathers, was stationed in and around New Brunswick during the Revolutionary War. In that time, he and his childhood friend Catherine "Kitty" Livingston composed a series of intimate letters to each other. Their suggestive wordplay fuels modern

speculation that their relationship may have been more than simple fondness, but any notion of a romantic affair is conjecture. There's no evidence that Alexander and Kitty even came into contact again after the war.

Still, the New Brunswick campus legend purports that the gray lady of Old Queens is Catherine herself, drawn to the spot where her paramour wrote his final passionate letters to her. She waits for his return, her gray face peering out the window, heartbroken and longing for her lost love.

The large iron gate at the entrance to Will's Way and Old Queens on Hamilton Street is the unlikely source of another local legend. It was erected in 1904 as a gift from the class of 1902, and superstition holds that a student who passes through the gate twice during his or her time at Rutgers may not graduate in four years.

As a result, hopping the low walls next to the entrance or taking the long way around Old Queens to avoid the walkway entirely has been a popular tradition for decades. Recently, the school has popularized the myth by guiding freshmen through it during orientation and warning them that next time they pass through should be at commencement, lest they risk the pitfalls of a delayed graduation!

Knights versus Tigers

There is a similar legend about another set of gates, but they're not at Rutgers. They're not even in New Brunswick. The iconic FitzRandolph gate that leads to the campus of Princeton University has a story that suggests accidentally passing through the center walkway will deny Princetonians a timely graduation. Sound familiar? This type of competing legend is hardly the only rivalry between the two schools.

Princeton is the fourth-oldest college in the United States to Rutgers' eighth. Just seventeen miles apart and chartered within twenty years of each other, their proximity created a natural rivalry. It may have come to a head in 1869, when the nation's first college football game was played in New Brunswick between the two schools. Rutgers won, solidifying historically hard feelings between the students of the two institutions.

Although originally represented by Chanticleer, a giant rooster, today, the Rutgers mascot is the Scarlet Knight. Princeton is known as the Tigers, with orange and black as the school's predominant colors. The two still compete fiercely against each other in various athletics, but the sports antagonism is just another battlefield in an ongoing war between the institutions.

A very old cannon has been the source of a different kind of contest for a long time. The historical facts about the cannon's origins are spotty, but as best as anyone can piece together, during the War of 1812, a functional cannon from a bygone era was placed in New Brunswick to assist in the fight against the British.

Mimi Omiecinski, owner of Princeton Tour Company, points out that the old British cannon "was built in 1670, making it one of the oldest weapons on display in the United States." The ancient gun was claimed by Rutgers students and remained in New Brunswick for decades until, Omiecinski adds, "One hundred Princeton Tigers gathered to return it to Princeton."

Eventually, documents emerged that confirmed the cannon, in fact, belonged to Princeton, so the heavy armament was brought home (with some difficulty) and planted in the ground on Princeton campus, buried halfway up its hilt at a slight angle. There it stands today. It's still a common prank at Princeton to earnestly engage freshman tiger cubs in a vain effort to "straighten the cannon."

While it has remained half buried in the same spot ever since the mid-1800s, it's not for the lack of Rutgers students trying to bring it back down the highway to New Brunswick. In 1875, an attempt to steal the cannon was unsuccessful due to its tremendous weight, so a smaller cannon was

A bevy of Rutgers students hauling away the contested cannon housed at Princeton University. *From* Frank Leslie's Illustrated Newspaper, *May 22, 1875.*

taken instead as a consolation trophy. After much ado, the lighter cannon was ultimately returned as well, but a new tradition was born.

Various attempts by Rutgers students to steal the big cannon have been foiled again and again over the years, including a 1975 caper that involved forged paperwork to obtain a security clearance. In 2012, independent filmmaker Zack Morrison's award-winning documentary short "Knights, Tigers, and Cannons. Oh My!" featured a history of the evergreen rivalry.

Today, the feud has mostly devolved into stunts like Rutgers students periodically painting the butt of the cannon scarlet red, with Princeton students retaliating by painting tiger stripes across beloved Rutgers monuments. The most prominent victim of Princeton's attacks on Rutgers is the statue of William the Silent on the Voorhees mall of the main College Avenue campus.

Coincidentally, "Silent Willie" is at the root of another urban legend at Rutgers. The original charter for Queens College was secured thanks to leaders of New Brunswick's Dutch First Reformed Church, who required a school for the education of ministerial candidates. Installed in 1928 as a monument to this heritage of the university, the statue of William I, Prince of Orange, reminds viewers of the significance of this national hero of the Netherlands.

Of course, the tongue-in-cheek story is that "Still Bill" will whistle at the virgin seniors who pass him by on their way to class. He's apparently earned his nickname since he's never uttered a sound!

The Rutgers Secret Society

A number of notables have graduated from Rutgers over the years. In modern times, HBO celebrities James Gandolfini, the actor who played Tony Soprano on *The Sopranos*, and Kristin Davis, the actress who starred as the supporting lead Charlotte on *Sex and the City*, both graduated from Rutgers. Professional athletes like football stars Ray Rice and Brian Leonard also got their start on the gridiron at Rutgers. Author Junot Díaz even penned Rutgers as the setting for his Pulitzer Prize–winning novel, *The Brief Wondrous Life of Oscar Wao*.

For as much talent as the school graduates each year, though, perhaps the most historically significant alumni is the celebrated scholar, athlete, performer and political activist Paul Robeson. Acclaimed at Rutgers for

The celebrated Rutgers scholar, athlete, performer and activist Paul Robeson. *Portrait by Winold Reiss, from the New York Public Library Digital Collections.*

being the valedictorian of the class of 1919 and the school's first Black football player, over the course of his long and varied career, he would become a renowned actor and singer. He ultimately used his platform to fight for social justice, believing that with his fame came a responsibility to advocate for his progressive values.

According to legend, despite his numerous accolades, Robeson claimed that his greatest accomplishment at Rutgers was to be "tapped" by the secretive Cap and Skull organization. Cap and Skull is similar to the secret societies of other venerable universities like the Flat Hat Club, founded in 1750 at William and Mary College in Virginia, which holds the distinction of being the first collegiate secret society in the United States. Skull and Bones, the notorious senior society at Yale University, has likewise seen members ascend to prominent positions in government and business.

Rutgers' Cap and Skull was established in 1900 by a group of ten ambitious seniors to unite the top leaders of their graduating class. They developed a process of initiation to carry on their work after graduation, and the method has continued for more than 120 years.

Due to its secretive nature, many of the club's traditions are still shrouded in mystery. Little is known, for instance, about the process used to identify and select who will become the next members of the exclusive honors society. Still, as an organization recognized by the college to some extent, some details are public.

Built on the pillars of spirit, history and tradition, the club boasts the motto *Spectemur Agendo* ("Let us be judged by our actions"). At one time, initiation was as simple as a physical tap on the shoulder. The process has changed over the years, though, and today the annual "Tap Day" ceremony formally inducts eighteen new recruits into the ranks.

Dressed in robes, the honorees solemnly sign a book that contains the signatures of all previous Cap and Skull members, a symbolic nod to their historic roots. The organization then publishes their names to the public, adding to an ever-growing record of what has become the mysterious upper echelon of student leadership at Rutgers.

The Lady in the Lake

Douglass College was originally known as the New Jersey College for Women. Founded in 1918, the school was renamed in 1955 to honor the efforts of the school's spearheading champion, Mabel Smith Douglass. Smith Douglass worked to overcome institutional and social barriers and create a space for women in higher education at a time when women were not afforded the same rights as men.

The school focused on technical training for jobs like nurses, secretaries, social workers and librarians. Under Smith Douglass's leadership as the school's first dean, enrollment increased and the college developed a well-regarded reputation for producing competent graduates. The work of Mabel Smith Douglass is rightly celebrated. Sadly, her mysterious and controversial death is another topic of interest in her life story.

After a number of personal calamities that included the untimely loss of her husband in 1917 and the suicide of her son in 1923, Smith Douglass resigned from her position at the college due to poor health in 1932. Likely suffering from depression, she was diagnosed with a nervous condition during her stay at a mental health facility. After her release, she took a trip with her daughter Edith to a vacation property the family owned on Lake Placid in upstate New York.

On the last day of their retreat, Mabel rowed a small boat to an isolated part of the lake, tied herself to an anchor and toppled into the frigid water. Her disappearance was determined to be an accidental drowning. Years later, Edith, too, would commit suicide, marking the end of their tragic family line.

That might have been the end of Mabel Smith Douglass's story, but in 1963, a team of divers exploring the bottom of Lake Placid encountered an incredible discovery. The cold and steady temperature at the bottom of the lake, the relative stillness of the deep water and the alkaline acidity of the water had resulted in a scientifically possible yet highly improbable anomaly.

Mabel Smith Douglass's body had remained entirely intact and undisturbed for thirty years. Due to the unique conditions of the lake, her corpse underwent the rare process of saponification, a chemical change that transforms body fat into a waxy material with a texture similar to soap or cheese.

When the divers discovered Smith Douglass, they said she bore the appearance of a mannequin or a wax statue. Before they attempted to bring her to the surface, where she partly disintegrated, she had been perfectly preserved, her delicate features fixed in a tranquil gaze, her appearance the same as it had been on the day she died.

The retrieval of the body and the subsequent investigation are outlined in the book *A Lady in the Lake: The True Account of Death and Discovery in Lake Placid*, by George Christian Ortloff. Through interviews and police reports, Ortloff pieces together the story of Douglass's final days and hours. He details the recovery of her body and how officials finally solved the mystery of her identity more than three decades later. Ultimately, with no surviving relatives, officials at Douglass College managed the funeral arrangements for the remains.

Today, rumors of the spirit of a drowned woman haunting Lake Placid persist, with a small body of literature dedicated to ghost stories about her.

Ghosts and Hauntings

Mabel Smith Douglass may not haunt Rutgers, but there are plenty of ghost stories on the campus named for her. In fact, Douglass campus may be the most reportedly haunted area of New Brunswick.

The ghost of Mary Putnam Woodbury Neilson lingers in her namesake building, where fresh bouquets of roses are doomed to wilt. *Photograph of portrait by Carl Ludwig Brandt, circa 1871, taken by Ira W. Martin, courtesy of the Frick Art Reference Library.*

Residents of Jameson Hall are often surprised to learn about a secret tucked away in the basement of their own dormitory. An abandoned swimming pool in the building's lowest level was available for students to use at one point, but legend has it that after an accidental drowning, the water was emptied and the doors to the facility were locked.

Curious students who have gained entrance to the empty pool have noted a creepy feeling as they explore the space where students used to congregate for fun. Some have even said that the spot is haunted, claiming they've encountered the ghost of the drowned victim on late-night excursions to the basement.

Before it was donated to Rutgers University, the Woodbury Bunting-Cobb residence hall was the home of its namesake, Mary Putnam Woodbury Neilson. She worked in her life to help establish the first free circulating library in New Jersey in 1883.

Woodbury Neilson's large rose bed garden was a source of great pride, but in the property shuffle that occurred after her husband's death, the house was donated to Rutgers and the school decided to rip out the roses. Mary was disappointed, to say the least, and she never forgave the insult.

Apparently, the woman could hold a grudge. Today, the spot where the garden once stood on the south side of the property is occupied by the A-wing of Woodbury Hall. As the story goes, whenever a bouquet of roses is brought into this part of the building, Mary takes her vengeance. They always seem to wither and die, wilting much faster than flowers that thrive in other parts of the building.

To say that theater director Jane Inge was devoted to her job is a bit of an understatement. Not only did she work in the Little Theatre on Douglass campus from the 1920s to the 1950s, but she also actually lived in an apartment above it until the day she died. Such passion and devotion are strong sentiments that have been known to energize a space and create an imprint on the surrounding environment. The strong belief is that despite leaving this world, Professor Inge has never left the building.

During her tenure, she was known for flicking the light switch on and off to attract the attention of her boisterously engaged students. To this day, the lights will inexplicably flicker during rehearsals (though never a performance) despite countless electricians inspecting the system over the years.

Her ghostly apparition has even been known to make an appearance to directors and students alike, a white dress billowing behind her as she crosses the catwalk above the stage.

RUTGERS RARITIES

Urban legends like these and other reports of paranormal activity were the subject of investigations by a team of paranormal investigators who named themselves after the institution where their love of the supernatural was born. Graduate students at the time Jessica Shea (née Teal) and Ray Brennan formed the "Rutgers Rarities" duo in the early 2000s after hearing more than a few strange stories from classmates.

Campus sightings of UFOs, ghosts and elusive cryptids like Bigfoot, the Jersey Devil and even a unicorn encouraged them to keep digging. "There were just too many weird stories to ignore," says Shea, "so by the time we started a website, we were already documenting a lot of activity. After we started to get some press, that's when people really began to reach out to us." Although their work has been paused for some time, the unique collection of stories is still available online through the Rutgers Rarities website.

Like real-life versions of the fictional characters Mulder and Scully from the television show *The X-Files*, Shea and Brennan worked to document urban legends, hauntings and any other sort of supernatural activity that came across their desks. From an interview with a SLIder, the nickname for someone whose personal magnetic field results in "street lamp interference" whenever he walks down the street, to overnight stays in some of the more reportedly haunted buildings on campus, the Rutgers Rarities team compiled a mountain of evidence that unusual activity around the college was way more usual than anyone thought.

In the years since they were students, the pair have moved on to new phases of their lives. Brennan points out that while he is proud of the work they did, he was always the skeptic on the team. That is, he was until he experienced inexplicable sensations while doing a paranormal investigation of the unoccupied third floor of the University Inn and Conference Center on Douglass Campus.

"I'll never forget the doorknobs rattling in the room right before the feeling of my arm holding the camera being forced downward," he says. "The tape recorder started to turn on and off by itself. I can't rationalize that away." Whatever was with them that day clearly didn't want them to have any evidence of its existence!

At first, both investigators were along for their wild ride, and the two always worked well as a team. In the end, though, Rutgers Rarities remained Shea's pet project. Today, all these years later, she's the one who keeps hosting the website online. Unsure about when their treasure-trove of stories might come in handy, she anticipates that something exciting is still yet to come of her adventures at Rutgers.

She's hopeful that one day someone will come along and pick up the mantle where they left off. "There's still a lot to uncover," she adds.

Nooks and Crannies

Rutgers University is the beating heart of New Brunswick, its students the lifeblood of the city. Every fall, thousands of newcomers arrive on campus and begin the stories of their collegiate careers. Every summer, thousands of others mark the end of their time here by crossing the stage to receive their diplomas and adjust the tassels on their caps.

In between these bookend moments, Rutgers becomes the geographic center of the action, the backdrop setting for all of the learning, experiences and exploration in early adulthood that takes place over four (or sometimes more) years.

Although its footprint is sprawling and its reach extends far beyond even the borders of New Brunswick, Rutgers has become a large place that's full of the kinds of nooks and crannies that capture the hearts and imaginations of all the people who pass through.

Whether caught in snippets from the headlines of the *Daily Targum*, the second-oldest college newspaper in the country, or heard in passing while sharing a rumbling bus ride across three campuses, stories of daily life at Rutgers permeate the air and wait to be told again and again.

They are passed down from one class to the next until, one day, they become a fixture of the campus, a local legend for which no one is exactly sure how it became known yet, somehow, everyone also seems to know is true.

CEMETERY STORIES

There is a long and strange tradition in the United States of maintaining cemeteries as public spaces that, alongside their primary purpose of containing the dead, provide opportunities for recreation and fresh air. According to Sara Jensen Carr in her book *The Topography of Wellness*, before large urban parks existed in cities, their precedent "was realized in cemetery design in the mid- to late 1800s," with spacious areas devoted to pastoral scenery, winding paths and flower gardens amid the headstones.

She notes how people seemed to be dying to get in, with "stagecoaches often lined up outside them on the weekends waiting to enter for a leisurely drive." Today, most people seeking outdoor recreation look to parks or nature preserves and not their local graveyards, but these unique areas are still open to the public; for some, they still invite exploration.

Whether tucked between high-rise buildings and downtown developments, nestled in secluded pockets along the fringes of the city or even protruding from the middle of an active parking lot, New Brunswick's historic cemeteries are unique places to reflect on the echoes of the past. In these spots, one can pause and take refuge from the hubbub of urban life as the rest of the modern world goes rushing by outside the gates.

CHRIST CHURCH AND GRAVEYARD

The oldest cemetery in New Brunswick is also perhaps the one most well tended and inviting to passersby. The ancient iron gates surrounding the courtyard might appear foreboding except for the colorful signs inside that welcome strangers as neighbors and dispel any uneasy notions. The brick-lined pathway through the churchyard provides a tempting shortcut between Church and Paterson Streets.

Those in a hurry would do well to find another route though. Many have found themselves lingering longer than they intended after stepping into this space and discovering the small world that exists here outside of time. Open to the public from dawn to dusk, the cemetery manages to feel like a private oasis. As good a spot as any to rest or to enjoy a quiet lunch, ambling visitors might even enjoy a stroll through the garden.

The greenspace is touted as "a place of repose for the faithful departed," a gentle reminder that, despite the beauty, there are indeed dead souls buried below. Amid the weathered headstones, the grounds are lovingly kept clear of debris by a man named Carlos, a lone maintenance worker.

He picks up after the guests and helps to keep watch over the property. When asked if he's ever seen ghosts here, he smiles. He admits that when he's alone inside the church, he's heard loud, clear footsteps approaching. When he calls out, though, it's to no avail. Like so many who visit here, the spirits of the past here are simply passing through.

Christ Church is steeped in the earliest history of the city. Dominion over the land during the seventeenth century defined the colonial tug of war that determined which European powers controlled different parts of the New World.

The spot that would become New Brunswick was first inhabited by Native Americans through the late 1600s, when the land was purchased and used by early English settlers in 1681. Initially called by names referring to landmarks like "Prigmore's Swamp" or "Inian's Ferry," the town was finally dubbed New Brunswick in 1724 in honor of the British king at the time, George I, Duke of Brunswick-Lüneburg.

According to Richard H. Steele's historical discourse delivered at the celebration of the 150th anniversary of the nearby First Reformed Dutch Church, the landscape during this period was, "wild and uncultivated. Dense forests surrounded New Brunswick; the streams were unbridged; the settlements were widely scattered; the roads, with the exception of the main thoroughfare from New York to Philadelphia, were little more than paths

A view of the iconic 1773 steeple atop Christ Church. *From the Library of Congress.*

through the wilderness; and it had all the appearance of a new country." However, English settlement increased in the first half of the century and the number of Anglicans from the Church of England became much greater.

By 1742, the parish in Piscataway that had served the local population had become insufficient to meet the demand for services, so construction of Christ Church began on this side of the Raritan. Philip French, the largest landowner in New Brunswick, leased his property in 1745 at a nominal rate to build the new Episcopal church.

The document, which charges "one peppercorn a year, only if asked," is still on display in the Rector's Office today. In 1852, the church was dismantled, and the larger one that still stands was built. However, the new construction preserved the iconic 1773 steeple.

The adjacent cemetery is a physical testament to the history here and the people who lived through it. Located near the side of the church cloister, the well-preserved headstone of poor little Catherine Harrison marks the earliest documented burial in the graveyard. The two-year-old girl died in 1754.

Brigadier General Anthony Walton White, the revolutionary son of the White family who was born in the nearby Buccleuch Mansion and went on to serve as General George Washington's aide-de-camp, also rests here. He is buried near the door to the church sanctuary.

Another headstone honors Dinah, the longest-living person buried in the cemetery. An African American woman believed to have been enslaved by the Dore family, Dinah was born sometime in the 1760s but lived until 1866 to see the outcome of the Civil War and her own legal emancipation from slavery.

Civil War officers Admiral Charles Stewart Boggs and his son, Lieutenant Robert Morris Boggs, are buried here too. The elder Boggs survived the younger, who died during the Civil War in Harrison's Landing, Virginia. Their stories are just a handful of the numerous lives memorialized here in New Brunswick's oldest extant cemetery.

First Reformed Church and Cemetery

The First Reformed Church stands in the shadow of towering parking decks as cars zoom past on nearby Neilson Street. On an early autumn afternoon in the cemetery behind the church, though, one can become lost instead in the sound of the steady breeze rustling through the shade branches hanging overhead.

The setting stirs a feeling reminiscent of a time before the superstructures outside the gates, a time when the brown and weathered headstones that poke from the ground and look like the crooked teeth of a jack-o'-lantern were newly planted, straight and solemn.

The haphazard yard is tightly packed, as if the graves tripped over themselves to squeeze into place and got stuck that way. Leaves blow across the muddy grass and swirl underfoot as visitors tiptoe over toppled tombstones. In an unused corner of the yard, a pile of gravestones awaits some unknown fate.

Most of the permanent residents here were born and died sometime during the 1800s, just a handful before and a handful after. An overrepresentation of surnames contain the prefix "Van," a reminder of the significant Dutch heritage both at the church and in the city during the eighteenth and nineteenth centuries.

Although it was technically an English colony, a large number of Dutch settlers began to migrate from New York to farm the untamed land along the

The clocktower church and cemetery. *From the Library of Congress.*

Raritan River starting in the 1700s. Albany Street was named for these early settlers, arriving from as far upstate as that colony's capital.

These devout migrants initially held worship in their homes, steadily organized the city's first religious congregation in 1703 and finally built churches to practice their faith under the Reformed branch of Protestantism.

The first church in the area was constructed in 1717, but by the mid-1700s, there was interest in building a larger structure in a more central location. In 1765, Philip French, the same landowner who two decades earlier had granted land to the Episcopal Church next door for next to nothing, was an active member of the First Reformed laity.

Apparently still reluctant to sell his property outright but otherwise amenable to generous terms of lease, he rented a lot of land to the church for two thousand years, again at the cost of one peppercorn per year upon demand. The spot for the First Reformed Church and its cemetery was thus decided, and all of Philip French's seasoning requirements were well met.

The first stone church built at this location served its congregants until the Revolutionary War interrupted services. Shortly before the outbreak of the war in 1775, a prize bell was installed in the tower with a long rope hanging through the center aisle that was pulled to call parishioners to service.

When it became apparent that war was coming, church elders decided to protect their precious investment. Ahead of the arrival of troops in New Brunswick, the bell was quietly taken down and carried away in secret to the nearby Old Queens campus. There, the heavy thing was buried on a hill, with just a handful of people aware of the hiding spot.

This was probably a wise move. By 1776, the British had taken control of the town and began to commandeer whatever supplies they could. As a matter of course, they assumed control of all public buildings and repurposed a number of the structures for the war effort.

First Reformed Church was converted into a hospital. Considering the rudimentary life-saving techniques available at the time, this distinguished building may have been the site of fairly gruesome medical procedures.

Worse, though, the desecration of the beloved church intensified as the building was soon converted into a stable. Cattle and horses were herded within to shelter the beasts from the winter cold while the occupation held control of the town.

After the dust of the war settled, the church was restored to its intended purpose (bell notably intact and livestock removed). The congregation continued to grow to the point that people had trouble finding seats on

A view of the churchyard at First Reformed. *Courtesy of Special Collections and University Archives, Rutgers University Libraries.*

Sunday mornings. When the need became too great, the original church was dismantled and the cornerstone of the new church laid in 1811.

Sandstones from the old structure were repurposed and brownstone quoins on the corners of the building added as an architectural flourish. Observant visitors today may notice the playful arrangement of small rocks in the spaces between the stones. Legend has it that when the masonry work was in its early stages, rapscallion children had pushed a handful of pebbles into the soft mortar. The workers liked the idea so much that they continued to embed the decorative chips across the whole church façade.

The building was finished in 1812, at last big enough with a capacity of 1,100 to house the entire body of worshippers. The church stood at the center of the business district and the sprawling Hiram Street marketplace. Here, farmers and vendors sold their produce and wares every day of the week.

Thanks to the institution's close connections to the city's leaders, as well as the central location of the church, the city council agreed in 1828 to invest in the construction of a steeple clock tower on top of the church. The intention was to serve all the people of New Brunswick. With its handsome design and quality craftsmanship, the clock has remained one of the most visible crown jewels of the downtown skyline ever since.

The churchyard retains a number of notable burials from the city's storied past. Dr. Ira Condict was an early church leader and professor at Old Queens with a passion for theological education who worked to raise funds to construct Old Queens, the first building on Rutgers campus. As a learned and earnest pastor, he was well loved by his congregants. He became sick with pneumonia and died in 1811, unable to survive long enough to see the new church. He was buried beneath the walls where he had preached while they were simultaneously being dismantled.

James Schureman, a Revolutionary War Patriot soldier who fought in numerous battles and escaped capture by British forces, is also buried on the grounds. He would go on to serve in the Continental Congress, and after the formation of the United States, he was elected as a congressman from New Jersey to both the House of Representative and the Senate. Perhaps his most significant contribution to civic life, however, was his tenure as the mayor of New Brunswick until his death in 1824.

Records of the church show that another Patriot, Captain Adam Hyler, the privateer whose vast wealth accrued at the expense of the British may still be hidden somewhere in the vicinity of New Brunswick, was also buried on church grounds. The exact location of his plot is unknown, yet another mystery surrounding his strange life and death.

The central locality of the clocktower atop First Reformed Church served the whole community. *Courtesy of Special Collections and University Archives, Rutgers University Libraries.*

The same church records also indicate a mass grave of ninety-six veterans, two Native Americans and, strangely enough, a horse. Local historian and researcher Ann Alvarez of the East Brunswick Historical Society believes that these are soldiers who died in 1778 during the Battle of Monmouth and has worked to erect a commemorative plaque in their honor.

Finally, two family names that might be recognizable to Rutgers students familiar with their eponymous dormitories on College Avenue are also buried on church grounds. Reverend Jacob Rutsen Hardenbergh served as both the church pastor at First Reformed Church and as president of the university before passing away in 1791. His tenure serves as a marker of shifting demographics as the last pastor to preach in Dutch.

Theodore Frelinghuysen, another U.S. senator from New Jersey with ties to New Brunswick, also rests at First Reformed. His politics included vigorously defending the rights of Native Americans by taking action to oppose President Andrew Jackson's Indian Removal Act of 1830. During his twilight years, he served as president of Rutgers University from 1850 until his death in 1862.

WILLOW GROVE CEMETERY

After decades of poorly maintained boundaries, what were once three small adjacent cemeteries established variously throughout the mid-1800s are now collectively known by New Brunswick locals as the Willow Grove Cemetery. Running along Morris Street a short distance from the New Brunswick Free Public Library, the eerie property is maintained by the City of New Brunswick.

It's evident from the elaborate size of several monuments that at some point this was a resting place for the wealthy. Seven former mayors of New Brunswick are buried here, as well as a U.S. senator.

The final resting place of Kusakabe Taro, the nineteenth-century samurai who attended Rutgers University. *Photo by Mark Neurohr-Pierpaoli.*

For decades, though, its upkeep was neglected, and swaths of it have now succumbed to nature. Sporadic, half-hearted attempts to revive the grounds have periodically rallied and fizzled. Although a number of notable and historic plots are well maintained, the overgrown cemetery is filled with toppled tombstones and patches of tall grass waving in the breeze.

Toward the back in one secluded section of the forgotten graveyard are several stark white obelisks looming over the other headstones. They have been painstakingly engraved with Japanese kanji to indicate, incredibly, that a nineteenth-century samurai rests here.

New Brunswick's historic ties to Japan originate in the mid-1800s as that country underwent major transformations. For centuries, Japan was a closed-off feudal society that privileged its samurai class, an aristocratic warrior caste whose members dominated the military government.

Starting in the 1850s, however, young samurai sensed a threat to their own futures if their country didn't modernize to keep pace with a growing imperialist West. They organized a domestic movement to advance industrialization, constitutionalism, Western-style education and a modern army.

As part of the process, they initiated a deliberate cultural exchange with Western powers to increase knowledge and establish goodwill between their nation and the rest of the world. Although it was still illegal to leave their country, the first Japanese students arrived in secret to work in the United States toward completing a university education.

Among them was Yagi Yasohachi, a fresh-faced samurai hailing from Fukui City. Yasohachi arrived in New Brunswick in 1867 to learn English and attend Rutgers College. There he assumed the name Kusakabe Taro. A new identity was all but necessary to emigrate and remain undetected by authorities from his homeland.

Taro distinguished himself at Rutgers. Through his diligent studies in mathematics and physical sciences, he was the first Japanese person to earn an induction into Phi Beta Kappa, the oldest and most prestigious academic honor society in the United States. He was also the first Japanese student to graduate from Rutgers and one of only two Japanese students to first graduate from any college in America.

Unfortunately, tragedy struck before he could return to Japan to promote the values of Western education. One of the risks he faced in leaving Japan was coming into contact with diseases that he and his countrymen had never been exposed to before and thus had fewer defenses against. After contracting tuberculosis, he died shortly before his graduation on April 13, 1870, at a boardinghouse on French Street.

His bachelor's degree and Phi Beta Kappa key were awarded posthumously, and following a short funeral ceremony at a nearby church, he was laid to rest here at the Willow Grove Cemetery.

After his death, representatives from New Brunswick traveled to Fukui City to continue the cultural exchange, and the ongoing process has continued ever since. Today, New Brunswick and Fukui City are officially recognized as sister cities.

In a broad sense, the explosion of cultural exchange between the United States and Japan in recent decades might trace its origins to students like Taro.

One aspect of Japanese culture that has become popular here is traditional Japanese folklore, specifically the stories of *yokai*, a phenomenon Michael Dylan Foster describes in *The Book of Yokai: Mysterious Creatures of Japanese Folklore*. He explains that a yokai is "a weird or mysterious creature, a monster or fantastic being, a spirit or a sprite." He goes on to say, "One common characteristic of yokai is their liminality, or 'in-betweenness.' They are creatures of the borderlands, living on the edge of town, or in the mountains between villages, or in the eddies of a river running between two rice fields. They often appear at twilight, that gray time when the familiar seems strange and faces become indistinguishable. They haunt bridges and tunnels, entranceways and thresholds. They lurk at crossroads."

The tales of yokai in Japan are hyperlocal. They are provincial stories whispered like urban legends and hardly ever travel beyond the borders of the location where they emerge.

Offered here, though, is an old tale from Fukui City that Kusakabe Taro may have been familiar with. The story originates in the Edo period, which ended with the Meiji restoration that Taro helped usher in. It is shared in honor of the samurai son of Rutgers who died in a far-flung land and opened a door between two worlds.

The tale begins with a young woman from Fukui City who was afflicted with a curse. More likely, she had contracted an illness of some sort. In any event, she had become a *nukekubi*. That is, when she slept, her head would detach and float through the streets in search of prey.

Akin to a vampiric condition, this violent yokai (always an otherwise ordinary woman) initiates a chase and seeks to consume the blood of the unsuspecting people and animals it happens upon. Stories of young men fleeing the hounding creature back to their houses find support in the deep teeth marks in the wood observed the next morning on their gates and doors.

As it turns out, to suffer from becoming a nukekubi is akin to sleepwalking; the women it affects are seemingly unaware of their own monstrosity until it is made evident to them. Sadly, in the Fukui capital city case, once the girl learned of her nightly excursions, she was so ashamed that she asked her husband for a divorce, ritually cut off all of her hair to repent for her behavior and finally committed suicide.

Experts seeking a treatment for these unfortunates have noted that the disorder is hereditary and can be passed down to daughters who begin to exhibit symptoms as they mature.

The search for viable alternatives to suicide continues for those who do not wish to live dishonorably in a circus or a brothel. Some believe that eating the liver of a white-haired dog may provide a cure, as this is a common target of the yokai's violence. Others insist that moving and hiding the sleeping body will eventually kill the head, but this is not the preferred solution for many families.

POILE ZEDEK CEMETERY

The Poile Zedek Cemetery is tucked away in a secluded pocket of the city bounded by Joyce Kilmer Avenue on the one side and the Mile Run Creek that runs behind a row of Livingston Avenue businesses on the other. It sits between Reed and Elizabeth Streets in the neighborhood near the New Brunswick Middle School building and Memorial Stadium, where high school football games are still played on Friday nights.

The property is an active cemetery shared by Congregation Poile Zedek and Congregation Etz Ahaim in nearby Highland Park. Bisected by a walkway through the entrance gate on Joyce Kilmer, the left side of the cemetery is well maintained with fresh-cut grass and many lovely headstones carved in Hebrew, dotted with pebbles. This tradition honors the deceased by showing that the grave has been visited by loved ones. Some believe that the baubles help preserve the soul. Others say they help protect the grave from demons and other monsters.

On the other side of the walkway, an older section of graves significantly predates the formation of the congregations that bury their dead here. This smaller Baptist graveyard has been relocated a number of times since the early 1800s.

Adorning a tombstone with small pebbles is a Jewish tradition to honor the dead. *Photo by Mark Neurohr-Pierpaoli.*

The grass on this side is patchy, and the tombstones are nestled among tall trees that cast long shadows when the sun hangs low in the sky. Its entrance was formerly on Livingston Avenue, but that gate has been swallowed by nature and is no longer functional.

The first known Jewish settlers in New Brunswick include a man named Daniel Nunez, who served as justice of the peace in 1722, and a widow named Hannah Lonzoda, who lived here starting in 1750. The number of Jews in New Brunswick slowly increased throughout the 1800s so that by the turn of the twentieth century the Jewish population was about 280 people, or roughly 1 percent of the general population.

Around that time, an influx of eastern European Jewish people facing discrimination, anti-Semitism and pogroms immigrated to America. In the thirty years between 1897 and 1927, five synagogues were constructed within a few blocks of one another in the vicinity of the Hiram Square Marketplace and formed the heart of the New Brunswick Jewish community.

Poile Zedek, which means "doers of righteousness," was founded as a mutual aid society in 1901 in a private home on Hiram Street, and in 1905, it purchased a lot on Neilson Street. Construction of the synagogue began there in 1923 and finished the next year.

The stone and glass building in the Romanesque Revival style was added to the National Register of Historic Places in 1995 as the last remaining synagogue from that period. In 2015, an accidental fire ravaged the structure and gutted the building.

Today, the exterior shell has been preserved intact, but the rest of the structure has been transformed in much the same way as other recent downtown developments. The interior was demolished and retrofitted as condominium apartments that nevertheless accommodate the historic façade.

One common belief among Jews in eighteenth-and nineteenth-century eastern Europe was that ghosts haunted abandoned synagogues. The spirits were said to appear at night to lead prayer services, and if the living participated in the ceremony by reading from the Torah before the spectral congregation, their fate would be to die before morning. It begs the question of whether the former Poile Zedek synagogue qualifies as abandoned or not.

The older Baptist graves that have been relocated across from the Jewish plots stand in contrast to the well-maintained headstones of Poile Zedek Cemetery. *Photo by Mark Neurohr-Pierpaoli.*

Above: A Star of David on the iron gate of the abandoned entrance to the cemetery. *Photo by Mark Neurohr-Pierpaoli.*

Opposite: Access to the ancient gate from the Livingston Avenue entrance of Poile Zedek has been claimed by nature. *Photo by Mark Neurohr-Pierpaoli.*

In Jewish folklore, a *dybbuk* is the tortured spirit of a sinful man who wanders the world in a state between life and death. The spirit is known to possess and control women and speak in the dead person's voice, much like a puppeteer or ventriloquist. The ghost usually takes this opportunity to mock and curse bystanders or even to accuse the living of crimes.

Although in some tales the dybbuk bestows great strength or psychic power, more often than not the possession is just extremely painful for the victim. The word *dybbuk* means "attachment," and the monster apparently takes hold of the body through the external genitals and refuses to let go. Thankfully, an experienced rabbi may expel the creature through a complex ritual.

Elizabeth Ciccone, current treasurer of the New Brunswick Historical Society, reports an eerie occurrence that happened to her many years ago just outside the gates of the Poile Zedek Cemetery. In the twilight of a late afternoon, an unusual man in old-fashioned coveralls stood among the graves and held his gaze on her as she walked past the cemetery. Discomforted by his staring, she continued on her way and looked over her shoulder, only to find that he was all of a sudden in a very different spot than before.

It's strange he moves so fast, she thought, and she changed her direction to cross the street. It was then she saw that he had once again popped up behind another distant grave. *Why, that's not how people move at all!*, she realized. She ran home as fast as she could. To this day, she swears that she never again walked past that cemetery, and she doesn't even look at it when she drives by.

She believes that she encountered a ghost from the early 1900s based on his appearance. Perhaps it was the dybbuk himself!

Highway Memorials

Observant commuters may have noticed a strange monument on the northbound side of Route 1 just before crossing the Morris Goodkind Bridge. There stands an abandoned plaza with a crumbling obelisk at its center. It bears no indication for whom the memorial stands aside from the haunting legend, "Their Bodies Rest."

The trash of the highway blows across its steps as cars and trucks speed by. Though technically accessible by an unmaintained footpath, few are ever likely to risk their lives to visit the strange place.

The site was a former monument erected in 1930 to commemorate the seventy-four veterans from New Brunswick who died in World War I. Originally intended as a restful spot for contemplation, the development of the highway rendered the space obsolete. The original plaque honoring the soldiers was moved in 2000 to the more central location where Jersey Avenue and French Street split to form a park area.

One of the notable names included is that of Joyce Kilmer, whose posthumous recognition as a venerated poet is thanks in part to the persistent lobbying of his surviving family members to keep his memory alive.

Kilmer's most famous poem, "Trees," begins, "I think that I shall never see / A poem lovely as a tree." Coincidentally, the beloved tree believed to have inspired the poem is believed to have been cut down, sawn into pieces and stored in a warehouse somewhere on Rutgers campus. Others suggest that the pieces were finally carved into souvenir gavels and distributed among a bevy of Rutgers bigwigs.

The site of Kilmer's birthplace is a preserved house located (of course) on Joyce Kilmer Avenue, maintained by the city and mostly utilized for municipal purposes. Another of Kilmer's poems, "The House with Nobody in It," aptly describes the memorial homestead. "I know this house isn't haunted," he wrote, "and I wish it were, I do; / For it wouldn't be so lonely

The remnants of the World War I memorial as it appears today. The once idyllic location intended for quiet reflection and thoughtful repose has been rendered obsolete. *Photo by Mark Neurohr-Pierpaoli.*

New Brunswick's hometown poet Joyce Kilmer poses in uniform during his service in the 165th Infantry Regiment in World War I, circa 1918. *From the Library of Congress.*

Much has changed around the grave site of Mary Ellis. *Photo by Mark Neurohr-Pierpaoli.*

if it had a ghost or two." The Joyce Kilmer memorial is periodically opened to the public; otherwise, it is available to visit by appointment.

Across the superhighway from the abandoned World War I monument, the parking lot behind the AMC movie theater on U.S. Route 1 may not seem like a likely place for a historic grave site. In a city like New Brunswick that has been built up, knocked down, redeveloped and paved over so many times across many centuries, though, anything is possible.

What was once a lonely and scenic grave site has today been transformed into a modern-day roadside attraction. It provides the fodder for plenty of local legends.

In 1783, fifteen-year-old South Carolina heiress Margaret Vanderhorst Ellis of Charleston married the prominent New Brunswick Revolutionary War hero Anthony Walton White. After several years pursuing business ventures in Georgia and New York City, the two finally moved back to White's hometown of New Brunswick.

Margaret's elder sister, Mary Ellis, also moved to New Brunswick in 1790. The tight-knit family are said to have all lived together in a house on

Gaining access to the parking lot grave site to pay one's respects is difficult but not impossible. *Photo by Mark Neurohr-Pierpaoli.*

Livingston Avenue. As previously noted, Anthony White, who died in 1803, is now buried at the Christ Church Graveyard.

Mary died in 1828. She was buried on a farm property overlooking the Raritan River. Her sister was buried alongside her in 1850. The grave site has never moved, but the landscape has changed around them quite a bit.

Legend has it that Mary fell in love with a sea captain who had also previously served as an officer in the Revolutionary War, perhaps an acquaintance of her sister's husband. The captain sailed down the Raritan and out to sea with a promise to return one day and exchange marriage vows with Mary, entrusting her with the care of his beloved horse until he returned.

Every day, she would ride the horse to the banks of the river, hoping to see his sails on the horizon. Sadly, she died waiting. He never came back. Her grave was planted in a rural setting with a lovely view of the river so that she might continue her vigil for her lost love. Some even say she was buried with the horse!

The plot was originally sectioned off by an ornate wrought-iron fence. By the 1900s, the farm had returned to nature, and the graves were isolated in the woods. The property continued to change hands, and as the area developed, it was eventually paved over—all except for the grave.

For a number of years, the location was the site of the Route 1 Flea Market. When the market was demolished, though, the current-day theater was built in its place. Still, the grave was always left alone, elevated and fenced off, supposedly at the behest of the descendants of the family. There it remains in the parking lot today.

THE FINAL STOP

Perhaps it's unsettling to be in a place where the dead outnumber the living. Yet at the same time, there's comfort in knowing that one's fate is to rest there someday, too. As a symbol, the cemetery invites contemplation of the nature of life, death and the legacies we leave behind.

Those who came before are hidden in plain sight. Wandering the sacred grounds here among both decrepit headstones and elaborate monuments alike gives pause. That the dead are buried equally side by side serves to acknowledge the truth that everyone's fate is the same.

In New Brunswick, a city that has rapidly changed for as long as it has stood, this recognition can prove difficult. Sometimes individuals were unearthed and reburied with family members in other cemeteries. Local experts likewise note that entire cemeteries were relocated or even destroyed. For instance, a plaque on Handy Street near Feaster Park commemorates the fate of such Civil War veterans.

The question of where to bury the dead may have been decided over and over again throughout the years, but the process was not always as transparent or well documented as one might hope. Some graveyards have been abandoned and built over. In others, the tombstones are so vandalized or so ancient that they are now impossible to read.

Still, for those willing to visit these places, to investigate their history, the stories of those interred are there, inscribed in stone, buried just below the surface and, against the odds, standing the test of time.

Every tombstone tells a story—the permanent marker of an impermanent life. And though the passing of time takes its toll and some of the story may be lost in translation, the dead still have something to teach the living. The tales of the departed continue to wait.

THE WAY TO HUB CITY

As the historians Suzanne Gehlbert and Morris Kafka-Holzschlag shrewdly note, for as long as anyone can remember, New Brunswick has been called Hub City. It proves difficult to determine when the city's popular nickname may have been coined beyond that.

The very phrase conjures a location with centrality of place on the map. The Hub City today is a destination where the lives of residents, students, migrants, commuters and tourists alike coalesce to create a vibrant scene of excitement and hubbub.

Here, the pace of life is set in the day-to-day hustle and bustle of industry, commerce and enterprise, growth spurred by hard work and organized labor. Local institutions create impacts that are felt around the world.

Such prosperity is possible in large part thanks to the arteries of infrastructure that invisibly facilitate the movement of people and goods to and from the city. The seamless integration of the ways and means of transportation are one of the most visible parts of the hidden history of New Brunswick.

Revolutionary changes in the ways people move have been at the heart of economic development for centuries. The shape of New Brunswick emerged as the city became a critical transportation node going back to its earliest days.

As transportation technology rapidly advanced, a piecemeal system that included stagecoaches, steamboats and locomotive trains enabled people to travel farther and more efficiently than ever before. However, each form of travel was also fraught with its own unique kinds of peril that had a hand in shaping the lives (and deaths) of many.

Both history and legends have been passed down throughout the centuries, with stories proliferating in the wake of the ever-changing transportation landscape and spreading beyond the borders of the city.

ROADS AND TAVERNS

New Brunswick is connected to its neighbors like the hubcap of a wagon wheel, with many spokes poking from the center. With both convenient access to the water and a well-worn footpath first traveled by Native Americans trekking long distances that passes through, this spot along the Raritan River has always been a convenient way station for travelers headed from one place to another.

Today, highways like Route 18 and U.S. 1 allow direct access to and from the city, but these major pieces of infrastructure are just the modern iterations of other historic thoroughfares. In colonial times, several main roads extended from New Brunswick and connected the city to other towns. The oldest among them was the King's Highway.

A permanent corridor commissioned by King Charles II between 1650 and 1735, the King's Highway was a 1,300-mile logistical feat that ran from Boston, Massachusetts, to Charleston, South Carolina, along the same route that had already been traversed by Native Americans for centuries. The improved road provided a physical link from the northern British colonies to the southern ones.

The first local enhancements in New Brunswick were completed in 1686 by John Inian, an early settler who serviced a ferry crossing over the Raritan River at the foot of Albany Street. Although a well maintained road was a common good, Inian's efforts may not have been entirely altruistic. It led directly to his business!

Just one of several principal postal routes, by 1738 the path through the heart of downtown began operating as a stage road. Stage service on such roads was scenic but arduous. Drivers raced wooden carriages past farms, meadows and woods over the ruts, bumps and potholes that dotted the unpaved and often unmaintained roads; sore-bottomed riders commonly referred to the bench as a "spanker."

An illustration of Inian's Ferry from a description. Note how the road leads directly to the crossing. *Courtesy of Special Collections and University Archives, Rutgers University Libraries.*

When they weren't stuck in the mud, requiring well-dressed passengers to get out and push, these "flying machines" had a tendency to topple over at their top speeds. It wasn't uncommon for passengers to break a bone along the violent ride. It was a welcome innovation when springs were installed beneath the hard wooden seats and pads were affixed for comfort.

It took several days to arrive at one major city from another in this manner, so travelers must have had a good reason for undertaking the journey. Staying put was clearly preferable in most cases! Trips like these were made in a stagecoach, so called because the carriage ride was actually completed in stages. Exhausted horses were routinely exchanged for fresh ones about every ten miles or so at dedicated taverns along the highway.

These rest stations competed with one another to provide food, spirits and lodging for the weary travelers, sometimes contracting with stagecoach operators to provide exclusive service. Enterprising tavern owners might even invest in or outright own stagecoach lines.

The Indian Queen Tavern was established along the waterfront on Albany Street in New Brunswick sometime during the early 1700s. It was able to maintain strong business in the emergent hospitality industry for many decades, even operating as a modern hotel well into the twentieth century.

In August 1776, during the Revolutionary War, Benjamin Franklin and John Adams traveled from Philadelphia to Perth Amboy for a meeting with British general William Howe to conduct peace negotiations. They stopped for the night at the Indian Queen, but the tavern was nearly full. In an accommodation that was common at the time, though no more convenient than it would be today, Adams and Franklin had to share a bed if they wanted to stay the night.

Legend has it that a not very serious argument ensued as Franklin touted the benefits of leaving the window open at night, while Adams, afraid the miasmic night air might make him sick, preferred to keep the window closed. Adams wrote that he fell asleep to his companion expounding on his theories late into the night, with Franklin's voice carrying out the open window and drifting down to the street below.

After a fitful night of stealing the covers back and forth from each other, the subsequent talks with the British were fruitless, and the war trundled on. Who knows how a better night's sleep might have otherwise affected the outcome of the negotiations?

The Indian Queen operated as a hotel and bar at the foot of Albany and Route 27 well into the twentieth century. *From the Library of Congress.*

The Indian Queen Tavern as it stands today, relocated and restored to its prior condition. *Photo by Mark Neurohr-Pierpaoli.*

The Indian Queen Tavern still stands today, although it was moved from its original location. Now in Piscataway, housed within the historic East Jersey Olde Towne Village, many of the building's original features have been restored to a previous condition and preserved.

Some say the knocks and groans of the old house sound like footsteps of ancient travelers pacing the bedrooms upstairs. Others dismiss the noises as the usual settling of a creaky old building.

CANALS AND STEAMBOATS

Boats were a popular form of transportation as a reliable alternative to difficult overland routes, especially for the haulage of goods. Of course, this particular mode of travel was restricted to waterways. To overcome such natural limitations, industry had to devise an innovative solution.

A system of water canals was financed and constructed from the late 1700s into the first half of the next century throughout the growing country.

This extended the reach of America's connected waterways deep into the fledgling nation, penetrating into unsettled territory and allowing boats to travel farther into the interior than was ever before possible. At the height of the canal era in the United States, a person could theoretically travel from New York to Louisiana without stepping off a boat.

A canal is essentially a long, wide ditch that connects two bodies of water. Although it may seem fairly simple, the process of actually carving an artificial river into the landscape was difficult to engineer, expensive and laborious. Because of its well-placed location along the Raritan River, however, New Brunswick was a natural choice for such an investment.

The Delaware & Raritan (D&R) Canal was designed to cross central New Jersey and provide a more efficient, safer route for transporting freight between New York and Philadelphia. Starting in New Brunswick and ending at Bordentown on the Delaware, the path cut seventy miles across the state and provided a direct, two-way route to either terminus.

A twenty-two-mile feeder channel that drew water from the Delaware into the canal was also required. Upon its completion, the trip from New York to Philadelphia would be reduced from two weeks over the ocean to two days on the scenic, placid waterway through New Jersey.

The brawn of at least three thousand Irish laborers was required to dig the D&R's main channel and the feeder. In the early 1800s, political upheaval and religious dissent saw increasing numbers of Irish landing on America's shores even before the potato famine sent millions fleeing from Ireland in 1845.

This country was not particularly welcoming to them. Anti-Catholic sentiment fueled unfair stereotypes and prejudice, outright discrimination and even violence. Newspaper advertisements seeking workers blared the warning that "No Irish Need Apply."

The awful work of canal building was among the few opportunities available to marginalized Irish immigrants. Today, the City of New Brunswick maintains a link to Limerick County in Ireland through the Sister Cities organization to honor the shared history.

Building the canal was a task easier said than done. Construction began in 1830 and lasted for more than three years at a cost of nearly $3 million. Working conditions were difficult, to say the least. Most of the heavy labor was completed by hand using shovels, pickaxes and wheelbarrows. Men lived in crowded tents and suffered from a lack of basic supplies. Many wore rags tied around their feet while working in the pit without boots.

Food was poor, sanitation was nonexistent and disease ran rampant. The pay for such work was advertised at one dollar per day from sunrise to sunset, six days a week. Adjusted for purchasing power in 2023, though, the thirty-five-dollar average daily rate was hardly a living stipend.

Quite the opposite, actually. No one can say for sure how many died under the brutal conditions of the worksite. Cholera festered and killed hundreds of laborers in 1832–33 alone. Many of them were buried in unmarked mass graves at nearby Griggstown, Ten Mile Run and Bull's Island. It's even likely that some of these unfortunates were simply buried in the fields where they died, the hidden graves of unknown Irishmen now scattered somewhere along the banks of the canal. A granite monument taken from a lock in the New Brunswick section of the canal was dedicated at the Bull's Island Recreation Area on Saint Patrick's Day in 2003 in honor of their memories.

Despite the dark history of its construction, the official opening of one of America's busiest navigation canals was an auspicious occasion marked with a bit of fanfare. In the summer of 1834, New Jersey governor Peter Dumont Vroom and a bevy of additional dignitaries began the two-day trip along the canal. Their barge was met by cheering crowds at every lock, bridge and basin on the route, with a twenty-four-gun salute welcoming them upon their arrival in New Brunswick. The party was then accompanied by a brass band and paraded through the city.

For nearly a century afterward, much of the coal that was mined in Pennsylvania and burned in New York City traveled across New Jersey's "big ditch." Canal work like tending to the locks and bridges or driving boats was an industry that fueled economic growth for many decades.

In that time, a notable variety of boats passed through, from tugboats to luxury yachts and many types in between. Early canalboats were pulled by mules on the towpath running alongside it. Eventually, though, steamboats replaced the draft animals.

At the New Brunswick terminus, the benefits of the canal were evident in the activity of the shipyards along the water. The city became a regional center for trade and the transfer of goods among wagons, trains and the canal barges. Oceangoing vessels then sailed up the Raritan and exchanged their cargo with the canal barges, which would then carry new loads back toward the Delaware River.

The pace of life in the city was set by the schedule of activity on the water. Canalboats shipped out before dawn and settled for the night when the sun went down. Seasonal access to the canal saw increased movement in the summer months.

Shipyards with docks along the canal and the river were responsible for incredibly productive industrial output. Even the famous Rutgers chant,

A day in the life of steam boat operators on the D&R Canal. *Courtesy of the Hughes Collection, New Brunswick Free Public Library.*

Before steam-powered boats came into existence, canal barges were pulled by mules along the towpath beside the water. *Courtesy of the Hughes Collection, New Brunswick Free Public Library.*

Steam boats tugging barges along the canal. *Courtesy of the Hughes Collection, New Brunswick Free Public Library.*

"Upstream, red team! Red team, upstream!" was inspired by the crew team rowing up and down the river, where, unbelievably, a bobbing boathouse was accessible from the water.

Over time, use of the canal declined as other forms of transportation gained in popularity. After closing down for the annual winter freeze in 1932, the waterway never reopened again to commercial transport. Today, while steamboats slowly moving along the water may no longer be found, the D&R remains important to the community. The canal that starts in New Brunswick is maintained as the state's longest recreational area.

Walking along the towpath in the quiet heat of summer, some say they have heard the shouts of the doomed workers who built the canal. Others have heard the eerie songs of boat operators floating in the air above the water. Still others have reported hearing the distant braying of the mules once used to tug the barges along the water.

TRAINS AND TROLLEYS

Although canals like the D&R remained in use for several decades well into the 1800s, they were ultimately supplanted by railroads before the end of the century. Faster, more powerful, less expensive and logistically easier than steamboats, locomotive trains soon became the dominant form of transportation for moving both passengers and goods.

The impact of such improvements was felt locally. In a town whose economy was built around its waterways, the results were not necessarily beneficial. Shipping had been a bustling, homegrown industry that allowed many to prosper.

Farmers would sell their produce to merchants in Hiram Market, who then transported the goods in boats to sell in New York City, but this old-fashioned form of business faded away as railroads took hold. Once farmers could directly access trains farther down the line, the city market and its merchants, the shipyards and the dock workers all but disappeared.

Train travel has remained a fixture since its early days in New Brunswick. Within a few years after the completion of the D&R, the New Jersey Rail Road & Transportation Company built one of the earliest routes in the nation between New Brunswick and Jersey City at a cost of nearly $2 million.

Continuing in the tradition of celebratory pomp and circumstance, service began with a commotion on January 2, 1836. A locomotive named

Uld Hiram St Market Torn Down 1865.

An ancient view of the Old Hiram Street Market at the steps of the clocktower church. The building was torn down in 1865. *Courtesy of Special Collections and University Archives, Rutgers University Libraries.*

the "New Brunswick" pulled thirteen banner-strewn cars toward the city at the breakneck pace of fifteen miles per hour.

Passengers were treated to a feast at the courthouse at the end of their journey. It's interesting to note that a train bridge across the Raritan had not yet been completed, though, so to finish the route, passengers had to disembark on the other side of the river and ferry across until a rudimentary bridge was constructed.

Railroads continued to lay tracks for separate train routes. These lines would eventually connect to form the modern Amtrak Northeast Corridor route, which still runs through New Brunswick today. The growth of the line mirrored the growth of the country. By 1900, there were over 190,000 miles of railroad tracks crisscrossing the nation.

Starting in the mid-1800s, a burgeoning streetcar industry also laid tracks to move trolley cars from one end of the city to the other. Pulled at first by horses, electrification would replace the animals before the turn of the century. In the next few decades, local and regional transportation was facilitated by these trolleys.

The local route began at the corner of Huntington Street and Easton Avenue before heading to Albany and George Streets. It traveled along Throop and Commercial Avenues before ending at a railyard near North Brunswick.

In 1909, a bizarre series of events led the trolley companies to arm their drivers with guns to fend off attacks from the Jersey Devil, the legendary creature of New Jersey's oldest folktale. The beast had reportedly been making its way north in a statewide romp that started from his home in the Pine Barrens. Eventually, the terrifying initial reports of a monster heading north gave way to humorous and finally outright ridiculous newspaper stories.

Were they laughing *with* or laughing *at* the hundreds who believed they had seen a monster that winter? Either way, making contact with the Jersey Devil had become something of a popular phenomenon. With tongue planted firmly in cheek, the *Philadelphia Press* offered $30,000 for a capture—$25,000 for the Jersey Devil himself and $5,000 for a signed interview with whoever brought in the animal.

Walter S. Flynt of George Street in New Brunswick thought that he might have a shot at the payday when his son burst into the house and exclaimed that there was a large varmint in the yard. Armed with a broom, Flynt rushed outside, preparing as best he could in the few moments he had to subdue whatever it was before it fled.

His effort was more than enough. Unfortunately for Flynt, his devil that night turned out to be a very large opossum. Reports of such large vermin still exist today in New Brunswick, with the backs of some 'possums reportedly reaching the height of the garbage cans they enjoy knocking over to sustain themselves. In any event, it may very well have been Flynt's son who caught the business end of the broom that night.

Ownership of the trolley rails was volatile and continuously changed hands. While several companies operated various lines, it was a difficult and unpredictable business. As commuter habits continued to change, the last trolleys rolled through the streets of New Brunswick in the 1930s. Their tracks are likely still buried beneath the pavement of the modern roads through the city.

Train travel never subsided, though. In fact, it only grew. A small train depot on George Street accommodated the first train passengers, but more substantial infrastructure was required to support the ever increasing

Hanging out at the Old Penn Depot, circa 1886. *Courtesy of Special Collections and University Archives, Rutgers University Libraries.*

numbers of commuters. The New Brunswick Train Station that remains standing today was built in 1903.

Still serving thousands of passengers per day, the modern improvements added to the building since then do not detract from its historical details of the Colonial Revival architectural style. The station still serves as homage to the town's colonial past.

The modest brick façade expresses an understated functionality. Notable flourishes like dentil molding along the cornice and a row of columns supporting the wraparound colonnade boast a handsome design.

Inside, large windows allow light to stream in and fill the room from its high ceilings down to the well-worn wooden benches and create a welcoming space for travelers.

In the moments before a train approaches the station, the small room swells and bustles with chattering ticket holders collecting their belongings and double-checking the posted timetables. At the sound of the oncoming whistle, the remaining few holdouts waiting downstairs to finish their

PENNSYLVANIA R. R. STATION, NEW BRUNSWICK, N. J.
Pub. by Hammell Bros., New Brunswick, N. J.

The Pennsylvania Railroad Station in New Brunswick was built in 1903 to accommodate the increased numbers of people commuting by train. *Courtesy of Special Collections and University Archives, Rutgers University Libraries.*

cigarettes or purchase a coffee dash up the long staircase at the last minute. Finally, everyone empties onto the platform to board.

When someone misses the train and finds himself alone in the room, a strange, palpable feeling lingers in the emptiness of the space where just a few minutes before there had been quite a din. It's almost as if the one who remains is left to haunt the hollowed-out vestibule.

Alongside the main station, a brownstone bridge holds the tracks over Easton Avenue and allows cars and pedestrians to travel below. Mineral stalactites hang from the arch and drip water onto unsuspecting perambulators, a perennial complaint among those who spend enough time below the bridge to take note. Many have also noticed the "steps to nowhere" hanging over Little Albany Street, the remnants of a staircase that used to descend to the street.

Trains travel out of the city along the Raritan River Bridge, a historic span of twenty-one viaduct arches across the river. Its wide expanse offers a broad expanse for daring street artists with tags like "PK," "SPOCK!" and "DUTCH." Their graffiti work is a familiar sight from the Route 18 highway that passes below, with some of the art having already endured for decades. Area bridges like the historic Morris and Donald Goodkind Bridges on Route 1 and the Route 18 highway bridge above the Lawrence Brook provide similar canvases.

A rainy day view below the pedestrian train bridge over Easton Avenue leading to the train station. Note the puddles forming on the sidewalk. *Photo by Mark Neurohr-Pierpaoli.*

Industrial railways branch off the main line and spread through the city. In some places, overgrown tracks cut through neighborhoods, inviting exploration and stirring the imagination. Many residential areas butt right up against these busy tracks. Cargo freighters pass by houses with a fantastic racket.

Some residents complain about the noise, but others have begun to report a strange phenomenon that is gaining traction. In the most common version of the story, a train approaches from a distance in the middle of the night. Its *clacks* and *clangs* get louder and louder until the cacophony crescendos just outside the house. Suddenly, the noise completely stops, and a glance out the window reveals that there is no train to be found. The phantom locomotive appears to be a fairly frequent but otherwise random occurrence.

Of course, there is no shortage of tragedy on the tracks as trains speed from one destination to the next. Both accidental and intentional deaths occur along the rails with regularity. Even conductors have noted strange activity approaching New Brunswick.

In one story, the apparition of a woman with her back to the train materialized on the tracks in the headlights. She kept pace, flying ahead of the speeding train without seeming to notice the engine behind her. After a minute of disbelief, the operator blew the whistle, and the woman stopped moving.

Opposite: Aerial view of the Morris Goodkind Bridge. *Courtesy of the Hughes Collection, New Brunswick Free Public Library.*

Above: The overpass above the Lawrence Brook walking trail is a popular hidden spot for street artists looking to practice their trade. *Photo by Mark Neurohr-Pierpaoli.*

Above: Overgrown abandoned railroad tracks often pass directly through residential neighborhoods. *Photo by Mark Neurohr-Pierpaoli.*

Opposite: The steel and concrete girders soaring over Lawrence Brook provide a broad canvas for graffiti artists. The work is visible to commuters from Route 18. *Photo by Mark Neurohr-Pierpaoli.*

Within seconds, she turned around and lifted her hands in horror as the train overtook her. The operator applied the emergency brake and conducted a visual inspection of the train, but there was no evidence of an impact. The woman had vanished without a trace, and the train had to continue along its route toward Princeton.

COMINGS AND GOINGS

Much has changed since the earliest roads through New Brunswick were utilized by stagecoaches and horses. Historians have lamented the destruction of the oldest parts of New Brunswick to make way for the Route 18 Highway Project in the 1980s, but the decision was unsurprising in a city that is constantly meeting the needs of travel and transportation.

Since its earliest days, New Brunswick has remained a network node, a place where individuals converge and contribute to the city's rich tapestry of life, if only for a little bit. The city has always been conveniently located alongside direct access to the Raritan River, with the earliest postal route through the colonies cutting across the town.

After trolleys and railroads were introduced, and finally the highway expanded through the city to accommodate the manifold increased numbers of automobiles regularly driving through, a commuter culture was established that cemented New Brunswick's reputation as a regional economic hub.

Untold numbers of people have passed through New Brunswick for hundreds of years, and it has created the sense of a place that is always on the move. The population fluctuates from decade to decade as industries rise and fall, from year to year as new immigrants arrive and other communities disband, and even from day to day as thousands of workers and students reportedly double the number of people in the city by arriving in the morning and heading out every evening.

New Brunswick is a place where countless many have visited. Those who come here and continue through to their final destination, wherever it may be, carry a bit of the story of New Brunswick with them. This extends the reach of the Hub City's stories far and wide.

DEATH, POLITICS AND POWER

As the seat of government for Middlesex, New Brunswick hosts many of the county's departments, offices and facilities. This includes the Middlesex County Courthouse and the Middlesex County Administration Building, which houses offices for the elected board of county commissioners and the county clerk.

The modest but stately New Brunswick City Hall, home to local officials like the mayor and city council members, also stands nearby. The neighborhood likewise serves as the headquarters of several local, state and even national politicians, as well as nonprofits, community organizations and lobbyist groups.

An adjacent complex of lawyers, bail bondsmen, legal services and notary publics occupies the surrounding streets. It's not uncommon throughout the workweek to see people in business attire darting from one building to the next, having hushed conversations over lunch at one of the nearby restaurants or grabbing a coffee to go in one of the small businesses that caters to the administrative and political class.

While it's apparent that official power is firmly entrenched here now, it wasn't always the case.

A Place for a Courthouse

In 1793, the decision to move the county seat from Perth Amboy, the capital of the former colony of East Jersey, to New Brunswick was contentious.

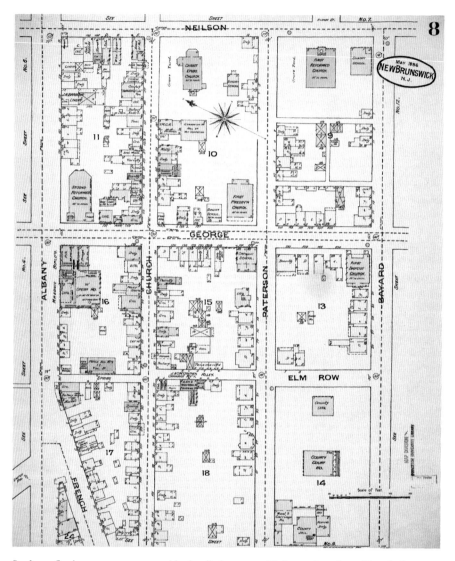

Sanborn fire insurance maps provide detailed structural information about historical buildings that may not be there anymore, like the former county jail in New Brunswick. *Courtesy of Princeton University Library.*

Passionate pleas and righteous refutations took place in the form of political broadsides distributed among the literate classes calling for the construction of a new courthouse in both cities.

Those in favor of moving the courthouse to the more centrally located New Brunswick argued that "Amboy is remote and inconvenient...illy qualified to

Taking leisure outside the county jail where public executions are held. *Courtesy of Special Collections and University Archives, Rutgers University Libraries.*

accommodate the courts" and complained that despite previously possessing the advantage of being a capital city, it did not become "respectable" and suffered from a "ruinous appearance." A flurry of retaliating replies were issued in response.

Perth Amboy clapped back by dismissing the "ungenerous" assertions. Petitioners rejected the notion that New Brunswick would become a "flourishing place," mocking the idea that "it may already be looked upon as the capital of East-Jersey." They directed attention instead to the financial burdens of moving the courts from a more well-established locale.

Despite the heated back and forth, the disagreement was ultimately decided by voters in New Brunswick's favor. The city's first courthouse was finally constructed in 1840 on the city block surrounded by Bayard, Paterson and Kirkpatrick Streets and Elm Row.

Sanborn fire insurance maps from the late 1800s show the county jail and an attached keeper's dwelling in proximity. It depicts fifteen-foot-high brick walls surrounding the property that contained a prison courtyard where public hangings took place.

In New Jersey, capital punishment was each county's obligation until 1907, when the state assumed the responsibility and began to use an electric chair for executions. Perhaps as a result of no longer requiring a gallows, a decision was made to put the space to better use. The adjacent courthouse park provided space for outdoor leisure. The Middlesex County Courthouse was expanded in 1913. In time, the entire block was demolished and reconstructed. The complex that stands on the same spot now was erected in the 1950s.

THE WHEELS OF JUSTICE

The wheels of justice have been grinding in New Brunswick for a long time. The question of who gets caught between them, however, goes back at least as far as 1867. The first woman to be hanged in New Jersey, one of the state's most notable public executions, took place here at the county jail.

THE ONLY CORRECT LIKENESS OF BRIDGET DURGAN: The fiendish murderess of Mrs. Coriel. From a photograph Taken previous to her execution.

The details of the trial of Bridget Deignan (often called "Dergan" or "Durgan" by mistake on account of her thick Irish brogue) were splashed across the headlines of national and even international newspapers. Her story was thrust into the spotlight at a time when anti-Catholic sentiment in the United States was at a fever pitch and public perception of the Irish was at an all-time low.

The only correct likeness of Bridget Deignan. *Public domain image by C.W. Alexander, via the Public Domain Review.*

Her conviction and execution served to solidify many people's opinions about the Irish, but whether she even committed the crime for which she was executed remains an open question to this day.

What *is* known is that a brutal murder occurred in the early morning of February 25, 1867, in New Market, Piscataway, New Jersey. Mary Ellen Coriell, a local doctor's wife, was stabbed to death in her bedroom with a knife from her own kitchen while her husband was away, assisting in the delivery of a baby. Fire was then set to the room in an attempt to destroy the body and any remaining evidence, but the flames failed to catch hold.

Mrs. Coriell's brutalized corpse was discovered the same night when Bridget Deignan, her domestic servant, fled the house and roused the neighbors. Holding tightly to the mistress's baby and trudging through

Left: The distance to the neighbors' house versus the time it took Bridget Deignan to trudge through the snow to awaken them was a contested fact in the trial. *Public domain image by C.W. Alexander, via the Public Domain Review.*

Right: The 1867 book *Life and Crimes of Bridget Durgan* depicted Bridget Deignan as a monstress. *Public domain image by C.W. Alexander, via the Public Domain Review.*

muddy snow, Bridget rightly believed her employer to be in grave danger. Soon, however, suspicion fell on the messenger, particularly because her story of the events that night changed from one telling to the next.

She initially reported that two men had come to the house early in the evening looking for the absent doctor and then returned later at night to burglarize the house. At first she claimed she did not know the identity of the men, but then she accused two locals whom she thought might have had a quarrel with the doctor. Later she claimed that there was a woman with the two men—or maybe two women were involved. Finally she admitted that she'd been threatened by the true murderers to not reveal their identities.

Bridget Deignan's life had been difficult up to her employment in the Coriell home. She'd fled the brutal poverty, famine and disease in Ireland that had taken the lives of most of her family. When she arrived in the United States, she felt fortunate to find work.

Five hundred people held special tickets for a closer viewing, but up to two thousand spectators crowded around the jail to witness the hanging. *Public domain image by C.W. Alexander, via the Public Domain Review.*

After her arrest, though, the time she spent in the New Brunswick jail may have been some of the most comfortable months she'd ever known. She was treated to regular warm plunge baths for the first time in her life, and donations from local women provided with finer clothes than she'd ever worn before.

Though illiterate and considered by some to be mentally deficient due to her thick accent and an epileptic condition, she was described by Dr. Coriell on the stand as a peaceable and trustworthy employee.

She maintained her innocence before and during her trial, but multiple "confessions" were alluded to in the newspapers that appeared to establish her guilt well before court proceedings ever took place. Had these pretrial references to a confession influenced the outcome of the case against her?

On the stand, prejudiced testimony from the prosecution's witnesses depicted her as a subhuman, animalistic fiend when it was revealed that the victim had suffered bite marks to her neck. This all but secured her conviction despite the otherwise admittedly circumstantial evidence presented in the case.

At her execution, copies of her so-called confessions were composed, printed and sold as souvenirs just outside the walls surrounding the gallows. City officials offered to sell rights to the confessions they purported to have secured. These conflicting accounts were mostly fiction and contained numerous unsupported facts, but they altogether served to justify the popular opinions the public already held against her.

On the morning of August 30, 1867, Bridget Deignan indicated that her conscience was clear, and she believed she was going to heaven. She approached her fate with grim determination, a rope dangling on her chest like a necklace as she approached the gallows. She wore a brown suit with a white collar and white gloves.

A boisterous throng of pushing, jeering, ticket-holding spectators had gathered to witness the spectacle. A loud cheer went up after her noose was secured and the cord of the mechanism was cut, jerking her into the air. The echo of their uproar as she struggled at the end of the rope reverberates outside the courthouse walls to this day.

A Great Place to Work

Steps away from the halls of government in New Brunswick towers another monolith of power: the Johnson & Johnson corporate world headquarters. A household name for well over a century as the company behind name-brand Band-Aid and Baby Powder products, Johnson & Johnson was founded in New Brunswick in 1886 by three brothers who pioneered the emerging field of antiseptic medical treatment.

Robert Wood, James Wood and Edward Mead Johnson brought together knowledge of the pharmaceutical industry, technical engineering prowess and the use of modern advertising techniques to form a small company that would go on to become a fixture of the Fortune 500. Although the reach of Johnson & Johnson has become global, the company never relocated its headquarters from small-town New Brunswick and still manages to maintain a significant local presence.

Before Johnson & Johnson's innovations in the mass production of single-use, sterile surgical supplies, about half of all patients who suffered through surgery later contracted fatal infections. The company's proliferation of pamphlets touting germ theory and other modern medical practices to remote parts of the country helped usher in a new era of medical treatment. By the turn of the century, doctors were no longer performing surgery in people's homes with unwashed hands wearing street clothes, but in hospital settings wearing surgical gowns and using sterile equipment.

At the same time, production of the world's first sterile surgical supplies began in New Brunswick in a rented factory building near the train depot. At first employing just eight women and six men, the business quickly grew.

Droves of immigrants arriving from Hungary provided a nearly constant labor pool for decades. By all accounts, Johnson & Johnson was a desirable place to work. Word spread back to Hungary about the steady employment, competitive pay, generous benefits and other perks like English language classes, and the proverbial floodgates of immigration from Hungary opened. It was common for multiple generations of the same family to be employed all at once.

As the company transitioned from privately held to publicly traded, the Johnson family developed a corporate credo in 1943 to guide both long-term and day-to-day business decisions. Alongside its shareholders and other stakeholders, the credo declares that Johnson & Johnson also bears a responsibility to benefit the health of humanity and to uplift its employees and the communities where they operate. "We must be good citizens," the document states, and "support good works and charities, better health and education, and bear our fair share of taxes." In a nod to its literal weight within the company, an eight-foot-tall, six-ton engraved quartz and limestone copy of the credo stands in the lobby of the New Brunswick headquarters.

By maintaining close ties to the local hospital infrastructure and the regionally pervasive pharmaceutical industry, Johnson & Johnson's influence has helped promote New Brunswick as the "Healthcare City."

A FAMILY CURSE

Although the company itself puts faith in its own corporate social responsibility as a self-sustaining model of good governance, successive generations of the founding family have notably been beset by scandal, controversy and tragedy. Enormous wealth has been passed down in the form of trust funds to the scions of the original brothers, but whispers of an inherited family curse have likewise pursued the Johnson descendants.

One branch of the family tree has been mired in inheritance squabbles and other controversy. At the age of seventy-six, John Seward Johnson Sr. married a thirty-four-year-old domestic worker whom he employed. Although he had established trust funds for his six children from a previous marriage, it was revealed only after his death that he had left more than $400 million to his young wife. A lengthy and embarrassing legal battle resulted in an out-of-court settlement that ultimately awarded $160 million to the Johnson children.

Terrible accidents and deaths have also plagued the family. Despite his enormous wealth and personal connections to the healthcare industry, Robert Wood Johnson Jr. died of cancer. His ironic parting words were, "I would give everything I have if someone could make me well." His son Bobby also died of cancer just two years later in 1970 at the age of fifty. The two men were the last Johnsons to work for the "family business."

Within a decade, two of Bobby's children tragically died in accidents in their twenties. Yet another son, Robert Wood "Woody" Johnson III, fell from an overpass and broke his back in a calamity that left him nearly paralyzed. Although he survived and would later go on to purchase the New York Jets professional football team, he suffered a permanent limp. Woody's daughter, a headline-grabbing socialite in her own right, also died young as a result of complications with her insulin medications.

The Johnsons' misfortunes are not merely a modern phenomenon. In 1922, one of the most gruesome crimes to ever take place in the New Brunswick community occurred in the orbit of Frances Stevens Hall, a wealthy Johnson heiress—and a prime suspect in the case. The infamous Hall-Mills murders inspired a media frenzy, with the spotlight shining directly on the close-knit community.

On the outskirts of New Brunswick, just over the border between Middlesex and Somerset Counties along a dirt farm road, there was a secluded but popular lovers' lane where couples were known to frequent for late-night trysts. It was here on the quiet late summer morning of September 16 that one young couple made a terrible discovery.

REV. EDWARD HALL   MRS. ELEANOR MILLS

The haunting gazes of the victims, Reverend Edward Hall and the choir singer Eleanor Mills. *Public domain image, via Wikimedia Commons.*

The bodies of two people, a man and a woman, lay side by side beneath a crabapple tree. Both had gunshot wounds inflicted to their heads. The man's face was covered by his hat. Beneath the bloody scarf wrapped around the woman's neck, her throat had been slit from ear to ear, her tongue and vocal cords removed.

The bodies were deliberately posed, the woman's head resting on the man's arm and her hand placed on his thigh. A stack of torn love letters was strewn across the two bodies. The man's business card was propped against his shoe.

The identity of the victims was quickly learned. He was Reverend Edward Hall, a popular and well-respected minister of the Church of St. John the Evangelist on George Street. She was Eleanor Mills, a soprano in the church choir.

Top: The parade of curious onlookers destroyed physical evidence at the crime scene. *Courtesy of New Brunswick Free Public Library.*

Bottom: The media circus that followed in the wake of the crowds sustained the public's interest in the mystery for months. *Courtesy of New Brunswick Free Public Library.*

Both were married, but not to each other. Reverend Hall's wife was Frances Hall Stevens, a prominent member of the community. As a member of the Johnson brood, she was the inheritress of a large fortune. Eleanor was the wife of James Mills, the custodial sexton at St. John's.

The families all knew one another through the church. However, both surviving spouses denied any knowledge of the affair that had been carried on for several years. Nevertheless, the illicit relationship appeared to be an open secret among the rest of the church congregation.

The Hall-Mills murders remain one of the most puzzling and notorious cold cases in American history. *From the* New York Daily News, *December 4, 1926.*

Within hours, the crime scene and much of the evidence it contained was destroyed as curious onlookers who heard about the double homicide descended on the farm where the bodies were found. They picked over the area for any memorabilia related to the crime. The crabapple tree, for instance, was stripped of all its branches.

Over the next few weeks, a media circus of hundreds of reporters arrived to gather the accounts of anyone with a remote connection to the victims. Within a month, the stream of constant visitors to the site was strong enough to support a row of refreshment vendors and souvenir hawkers who set up shop nearby and did strong business. Whatever physical evidence there had been was trampled beneath thousands of feet like a fairgrounds.

Although public interest in the story was intense and fueled by speculation and scrutiny in the newspapers, the investigation faltered as jurisdiction over the case remained unclear and no plausible leads emerged. A grand jury was finally convened, but after a review of the evidence and witness testimony gathered through subpoena, there were no indictments.

Four years later, the story was thrust back into the news as new details and allegations emerged. Mrs. Hall Stevens, two of her relatives and her driver were identified as suspects in the murders, and they were arrested in the middle of the night.

On trial, humiliating and intimate details of the salacious affair were brought to light. The outrageous and unreliable testimony of "the pig woman," a bed-ridden swine farmer who claimed to have knowledge of the murders proved to be the climax of the trial.

However, Stevens Hall's "billion dollar defense" team successfully managed to convince a jury that she was innocent. After her acquittal for the murder of her husband, which was tried separately, all of the remaining charges were dropped.

Frances Stevens Hall continued to live in her stately New Brunswick home until the natural end of her life, but she never spoke publicly about the murders again. Both she and her husband are now buried together at Brooklyn, New York's Greenwood Cemetery. Eleanor Mills, alongside her husband and daughter, is buried at Van Liew Cemetery in North Brunswick.

Although at the time many believed that Frances Stevens Hall's wealth allowed her to buy her way out of jail, many modern interpretations concur with the jury that the mishandled evidence and dubious testimony introduced throughout the trial were not strong enough for a conviction.

Conjecture over who actually committed the heinous crimes lingers, and the Hall-Mills murders remain one of the most puzzling and notorious cold cases in American history.

Two Women, Two Fates

The main stories in this chapter are of two women from New Brunswick, each accused of horrible crimes. Both were shamefully dragged through the press and judged mercilessly in a court of public opinion well before their trials. The stark divergence in their fates, however, reveals the disparities of the justice system.

On the one hand, Bridget Deignan was railroaded through the courts, convicted and sentenced to death in a matter of weeks based on her ethnicity and the unfortunate circumstance of her proximity to a murder. Prosecutors failed to identify any substantial physical evidence to even suggest her involvement.

On the other hand, despite strong motive and ample opportunity, it took four years to indict Frances Stevens Hall, and she was ultimately acquitted. Her prominence and wealth helped to establish her as a very different kind of woman on trial before a jury of her peers. As such, the outcome was radically different.

This is not to argue that either woman deserved to be found guilty. Although the world may never know what really happened in either case, it's just as likely that one woman was as innocent as the other. The main differences between them were the preconceived notions that others held about them based on social and economic statuses.

The lessons of their stories continue to whisper down the corridors and through the halls of power. The ghosts of inequity linger in the shadows of the courtroom.

BIBLIOGRAPHY

Access Genealogy. "Delaware Indian Tribe Clans." https://accessgenealogy. com/delaware/delaware-indian-tribe-clans.htm.

Adams, Richard C. *Legends of the Delaware Indians and Picture Writing*. N.p.: Pantianos Classics, 1905.

An Address to the Electors of the County of Middlesex. A call to civilly end the disagreement between New Brunswick and Perth Amboy. Signed "A Friend to New Jersey." 1793. Rutgers University Libraries Special Collections & University Archives.

The Adirondacks. "The Lady in the Lake: One of the Adirondacks' Most Compelling Mysteries." https://www.adirondack.net/history/lady-in-the-lake.

Alvarez, Ann. "The Mass Grave at the First Reformed Church, New Brunswick, N.J." 2008. https://search.worldcat.org/title/mass-grave-at-the-first-reformed-church-new-brunswick-nj/oclc/968225152.

———. "The Mystery of the Inscribed Rocks & Tunnel." East Brunswick Historical Society, May 19, 2019. Slideshow presentation.

American Hungarian Foundation. https://www.ahfoundation.org/about-the-foundation.

Anolik, Ruth B. "Appropriating the Golem, Possessing the Dybbuk: Female Retellings of Jewish Tales." *Modern Language Studies* 31, no. 2 (Autumn 2001): 39–55. https://doi.org/10.2307/3195336.

Balassa, Iván, and Gyula Ortutay. *Hungarian Ethnography and Folklore*. Translated by Maria Bales and Kenneth Bales N.p., 1979. https://mek. oszk.hu/02700/02790/html/index.html.

Barber, John W., and Henry Howe. *Historical Collections of the State of New Jersey*. N.p.: Creative Media Partners, LLC, 2016.

Beetham, Sarah. "When Memory Fails, Part 2: Answers." 2016. https://sarahbeetham.com/2016/06/06/when-memory-fails-part-2-answers.

Belle, Kelly, and Tom Belle. "New Brunswick's White House: The Buccleuch Mansion." The History Girl, 2014. https://www.thehistorygirl.com/2014/03/buccleuch-mansion-new-brunswick-nj.html.

Benedict, William H. *New Brunswick in History*. St. Berwyn Heights, MD: Heritage Books, 2013.

———. "The Nine Roads of New Brunswick." *Proceedings of the New Jersey Historical Society* 14 (1929): 163–80.

Biography. "Thomas Paine Biography." 2021. http://www.biography.com/people/thomas-paine-9431951.

Bonner, William H. "Cooper and Captain Kidd." *Modern Language Notes* 61, no. 1 (1946): 21–27. https://doi.org/10.2307/2910254.

Boucher, Bernadette A., and Robert Belvin. *Cemeteries in New Brunswick*. New Brunswick Free Public Library Archive, 1999.

Boyd, Kendra, Marisa J. Fuentes, Deborah G. White and Miya Carey, eds. *Scarlet and Black*. Vol. 2, *Constructing Race and Gender at Rutgers, 1865–1945*. New Brunswick, NJ: Rutgers University Press, 2020.

Britannica. "Algonquian Languages." 2017. https://www.britannica.com/topic/Algonquian-languages.

———. "Canals and Inland Waterways." https://www.britannica.com/technology/canal-waterway/United-States.

———. "Raritan River." 2020. https://www.britannica.com/place/Raritan-River.

———. "Samurai | Meaning, History, & Facts." 2024. https://www.britannica.com/topic/samurai.

Canal Society of New Jersey. "Delaware and Raritan Canal." https://canalsocietynj.org/canal-history/delaware-and-raritan-canal.

Cap & Skull. "Register of Skulls." http://capandskull.org/#!/skulls.

Carr, Sara J. *The Topography of Wellness: How Health and Disease Shaped the American Landscape*. Charlottesville: University of Virginia Press, 2021.

Cawley, George. "Canal Boat Wreck on the D&R." *On the Level*, no. 140 (May 2022): 1–2.

Central New Jersey Home News. "Bagonye's Chapel Is Weirdly Fitted Up for His Séances with Spirits." April 22, 1921.

———. "Paid $80 to Be Cured by 'Evil Spirits.'" October 7, 1915.

———. "Witchcraft Believers Weaken Before Priest's Long Talk." October 4, 1936.

———. "Woman Accused of Witchcraft Turns Tables on Her Enemies." October 2, 1936.

Chi, Sheena. "Statue of Cardinal Mindszenty, New Brunswick, NJ." Flickr. https://www.flickr.com/photos/sheenachi/4124604407.

Christ Church New Brunswick. "History of Christ Church." https://www.christchurchnewbrunswick.org/history-of-the-parish.

City of New Brunswick. "City History." https://www.cityofnewbrunswick.org/visitors/history/index.php.

The City of New Brunswick, New Jersey: Its History, Its Homes & Its Industries. New Brunswick, NJ: Daily Times, 1908. https://archive.org/details/cityofnewbrunswi00unse/page/n5/mode/2up.

Clark, Richard. "American Female Hangings, 1632 to 1937." Capital Punishment UK. https://www.capitalpunishmentuk.org/amfemhang.html.

Cohn, Deborah. "A History of Congregation Poile Zedek." Jewish Historical Society of Central Jersey, 2016. https://www.jewishgen.org/jhscj/NewsletterSpring2016.pdf.

Colleluori, Salvatore. "The Colonial Tavern, Crucible of the American Revolution." War on the Rocks, 2015. https://warontherocks.com/2015/04/the-colonial-tavern-crucible-of-the-american-revolution.

Collier, Jess. "The Story of the Lady in the Lake." Lake Placid, 2014. https://www.lakeplacid.com/story/2014/10/ghost-stories-story-lady-of-the-lake.

"Conveyance. Ahanderamock [tract of land on the South Side of Raritan River], Middlesex County." TO: Elizabeth Carteret (Lady) (Proprietrix). FROM: Canacamo; Indians; Quaramack (Sacamaker). 1681. In *Early Land Records, 1650–1801.* Liber 1, Part B (EJ): Folio 187 / 152 (SSTSE023). New Jersey State Archives.

"Conveyance. Middlesex County." TO: Cornelius Longfield (Merchant). FROM: Eschererk; Indians; Perkanouss; Queramacke. 1682. In *Early Land Records, 1650–1801.* Liber 4 (EJ): Folio 45 (SSTSE023). New Jersey State Archives.

"Conveyance. Raritan River, Middlesex County." TO: Cornelius Longfield. FROM: Eschapous; Eschark; Heromack (Sachem); Indians; Peckaoney. 1681. In *Early Land Records, 1650-1801.* Liber 4 (EJ): Folio 46 (SSTSE023). New Jersey State Archives.

Cook, Joel. *The World's Famous Places and Peoples: America.* Vol. 3. 1st ed. New York: Merrill and Baker, 1900. https://www.gutenberg.org/files/41776/41776-h/41776-h.htm.

Crossroads of the American Revolution. "Buccleuch Mansion—New Brunswick, NJ." https://revolutionarynj.org/storyline_photo2/buccleuch-mansion-new-brunswick-nj-2.

———. "Maritime Wars." https://revolutionarynj.org/stories/maritime-wars.

Cushman, Dustin R. "The Context of Death: Burial Rituals in the Delaware Valley." *Archaeology of Eastern North America* 35 (2007): 153–60. https://www.jstor.org/stable/40914518.

Dauber, Jeremy. "Demons, Golems, and Dybbuks: Monsters of the Jewish Imagination." American Library Association. https://www.ala.org/tools/sites/ala.org.tools/files/content/Jewish%20Literature%20Demons%20Golems%20and%20Dybbuks_0.pdf.

Daughters of the American Revolution, Jersey Blue Chapter. "History of Buccleuch Mansion." https://www.jerseybluedar.org/history.html.

Dean, Nora T. "Lenape Funeral Customs." Edited by Herbert Kraft. *The Lenape Indian: A Symposium, Seton Hall Publications*, no. 7 (1984): 63–70.

Delaware and Raritan Canal State Park. "D&R Canal—A Historic Place." https://dandrcanal.org/history.

Donnoli, Nick. "Through the Gates: The Myth Surrounding FitzRandolph Gate." Princeton University, 2017. https://www.princeton.edu/news/2017/05/30/through-gates-myth-surrounding-fitzrandolph-gate.

Duane, Sheila. "After 149 Years, Justice for an Irish Immigrant Executed for Murder." Irish Central, 2016. https://www.irishcentral.com/roots/after-149-years-justice-for-an-irish-immigrant-executed-for-murder.

———. *Bridget's Hanging*. N.p.: CreateSpace Independent Publishing Platform, 2016.

Duvert, Evie. "Haunted Rutgers." Rutgers University, 2019. https://www.rutgers.edu/news/haunted-rutgers.

Encyclopaedia Judaica. "New Brunswick." Jewish Virtual Library. https://www.jewishvirtuallibrary.org/new-brunswick.

Feldman, Evan M. "Kusakabe Taro." Rutgers Meets Japan: Early Encounters, 2020. https://sites.rutgers.edu/rutgers-meets-japan/kusakabe-taro.

Find a Grave. "Capt Adam Huyler (1735–1782)." https://www.findagrave.com/memorial/124911445/adam-huyler.

———. "James Schureman." 2017. https://www.findagrave.com/memorial/7751716/james-schureman.

———. "Theodore Frelinghuysen." https://www.findagrave.com/memorial/7474887/theodore-frelinghuysen.

First Reformed Church of New Brunswick. "Our History." First Reformed Church of New Brunswick, New Jersey. https://www.firstreformedchurch.net/history.

Fore, Samuel K. "Anthony Walton White." George Washington Presidential Library at Mount Vernon. https://www.mountvernon.org/library/digitalhistory/digital-encyclopedia/article/anthony-walton-white.

Foster, Michael D. *The Book of Yokai: Mysterious Creatures of Japanese Folklore.* Berkeley: University of California Press, 2015.

Fox, Thomas. *Hidden History of the Irish of New Jersey.* Charleston, SC: The History Press, 2011.

Frazza, Al. "Piscataway Historic Sites." Revolutionary War New Jersey. https://www.revolutionarywarnewjersey.com/new_jersey_revolutionary_war_sites/towns/piscataway_nj_revolutionary_war_sites.htm.

Freeport, Andrew. *Through a Perspective.* A refutation of New Brunswick's argument for the courthouse and a call to place it in Perth Amboy. Rutgers University Libraries Special Collections & University Archives, 1793.

Gallery '50 and Special Collections and University Archives, Archibald Stevens Alexander Library. 1997. "'Resolved that I Should Be a Man': Rutgers College Goes Coed." Gallery Exhibit Guide, Celebrating 25 Years of Women at Rutgers College.

Garman, Emma. "Behind the Johnson & Johnson Curse." Daily Beast, 2013. https://www.thedailybeast.com/behind-the-johnson-and-johnson-curse.

Geary, Rick. *Lovers' Lane: The Hall-Mills Mystery.* N.p.: NBM/ComicsLit, 2012.

Gehlbert, Suzanne L., and Morris J. Kafka-Holzschlag. "New Brunswick and Transportation: A Brief Sketch of the History of Transportation and the Architecture of the Train Station." *Journal of the Rutgers University Libraries* 50, no. 1 (1989).

Genovese, Peter. *New Jersey Curiosities: Quirky Characters, Roadside Oddities and Other Offbeat Stuff.* Essex, CT: Globe Pequot Press, 2011.

Ghosts of America. "New Brunswick, New Jersey, Ghost Sightings." https://www.ghostsofamerica.com/0/New_Jersey_New_Brunswick_ghost_sightings.html.

Gray, Ashlee. "Indian Queen Tavern." Clio: Your Guide to History, 2019. https://theclio.com/entry/75098.

Great American Stations. "New Brunswick, NJ (NBK)." https://www.greatamericanstations.com/stations/new-brunswick-nj-nbk.

Grodeska, J.F. "The Bloody History of Kings Highway." Jersey Shore Scene, 2022. https://jerseyshorescene.com/the-bloody-history-of-kings-highway.

Grumet, Robert S. *The Munsee Indians: A History*. Norman: University of Oklahoma Press, 2022.

Gurowitz, Margaret. "Hungarian University." Kilmer House, 2008. https://www.kilmerhouse.com/2008/06/hungarian-university.

Harlow, Alvin F. *When Horses Pulled Boats: A Story of Early Canals*. N.p.: American Canal and Transportation Center, 1983.

Harrington, M.R. *Religion and Ceremonies of the Lenape (Classic Reprint)*. London: Forgotten Books, 2012.

Harris, Harold J. "'Little Hungary': A Study of the Hungarian Community in New Brunswick [N.J.] and of Its Relationship to the Larger Community." In *Special Collections & University Archives Primary Source Highlights*. New Brunswick, NJ, 1949? https://speccol.libraries.rutgers.edu/items/show/573.

Harris, Vashti. "Local Historian Highlights Mysterious Rocks with Carvings in East Brunswick." Central Jersey, 2019. https://centraljersey.com/2019/06/25/local-historian-highlights-mysterious-rocks-with-carvings-for-east-brunswick-residents.

Haui, József, and Marcell Jankovics, dirs. *Hungarian Folk Tales*. Season 2, episode 7, "The Two Princes with Hair of Gold." Featuring Piroska Molnár. Kecskemét Film Studio, aired April 3, 2017. https://www.youtube.com/watch?v=Em03UdVqGJg.

Historical Marker Project. "The Canal Dug by Irishmen." 2014. https://historicalmarkerproject.com/markers/HMOPB_the-canal-dug-by-irishmen_Princeton-NJ.html.

Historical Society of West Windsor. "The Delaware & Raritan Canal." https://www.westwindsorhistory.com/the-dr-canal.html.

Hitakonanu'laxk. *The Grandfathers Speak: Native American Folk Tales of the Lenapé People*. Northampton, MA.: Interlink Publishing Group Incorporated, 1994.

House Speaker Biographies. "John B. Bayard." https://www.legis.state.pa.us/cfdocs/legis/SpeakerBios/SpeakerBio.cfm?id=70.

Hullfish, William, ed. *The Canaller's Songbook: Words, Music, and Chords to Over Thirty Canal Songs*. N.p.: American Canal and Transportation Center, 1984.

IndyFan222. "Railroad Ghost Stories: r/trains." Reddit, 2019. https://www.reddit.com/r/trains/comments/avfa27/railroad_ghost_stories.

Ingraham, Joseph H. "Story of Ghost's Midnight Visit at Buccleuch." *Sunday Times* (New Brunswick), December 18, 1932.

Janes, Erika. "8 Fun Facts About the Johnson & Johnson Credo." Johnson & Johnson, 2018. https://www.jnj.com/our-heritage/8-fun-facts-about-the-johnson-johnson-credo.

Johnson & Johnson. "Our Credo." 2023. https://www.jnj.com/our-credo.

Johnson & Johnson Our Story. "Our Beginning." https://ourstory.jnj.com/our-beginning.

Kanpai Japan. "Fukui—Capital of the Former Echizen Province." 2021. https://www.kanpai-japan.com/fukui.

Kaufmann, Susan. "Deciphering the Dead: New Brunswick's Willow Grove Cemetery." Hidden New Jersey, 2013. http://www.hiddennj.com/2013/10/deciphering-dead-new-brunswicks-willow.html.

———. "The Disappearing Dean and the Lady in the Lake." Hidden New Jersey, 2013. http://www.hiddennj.com/2013/06/the-disappearing-dean-and-lady-in-lake.html.

———. "Firing Up a Celebration of Joy in New Brunswick." Hidden New Jersey, 2015. http://www.hiddennj.com/2015/06/firing-up-celebration-of-joy-in-new.html.

———. "Franklin and Adams Slept Here: Indian Queen Tavern at East Jersey Olde Towne." Hidden New Jersey, 2011. http://www.hiddennj.com/2011/09/franklin-and-adams-slept-here-indian.html.

———. "The Japanese at Willow Grove Cemetery: Revealing New Jersey's Role in Modernizing a Nation." Hidden New Jersey, 2013. http://www.hiddennj.com/2013/10/the-japanese-at-willow-grove-cemetery.html.

———. "New Brunswick's Guest House: Maybe, Maybe Not." Hidden New Jersey, 2015. http://www.hiddennj.com/2015/02/new-brunswicks-guest-house-maybe-maybe.html.

Keansburg High School. "Story of the Seas." https://www.keansburg.k12.nj.us/khs/Keansburg/chapter_5.htm.

Kilmer, Joyce. "The House with Nobody in It." Your Daily Poem. https://www.yourdailypoem.com/listpoem.jsp?poem_id=197.

———. "Trees." Poetry Foundation. https://www.poetryfoundation.org/poetrymagazine/poems/12744/trees.

Kimmel, Richard J. *Ghosts of Central New Jersey: Bizarre, Strange, and Deadly.* Atglen, PA: Schiffer Publishing, 2010.

King, Albert C. "Medicine and New Jersey: Medical, Pharmaceutical and Health-Related Manuscripts in the Rutgers University Libraries." In *Special Collections and University Archives.* New Brunswick, NJ: Rutgers University Libraries, 1998.

Klett, Joseph R. *Using the Records of the East and West Jersey Proprietors.* Trenton: New Jersey State Archives, 2014.

Koennemann, Kristen. "The Oldest Road in America, the King's Highway, Passes Right through New Jersey." OnlyInYourState, 2023. https://www.onlyinyourstate.com/new-jersey/kings-highway-nj.

Krykew, Sarah. "Lenni Lenape: Dreams, the Art of Healing, and Death & Burial Practices." Chadds Ford Historical Society, 2016. https://chaddsfordhistorical.wordpress.com/2016/07/28/lenni-lenape-dreams-the-art-of-healing-and-death-burial-practices.

Laden, Greg. "Whale, Croc, Lost in Brazil." Comment by Brian Switek about the whale legend on Science Blogs, 2007. https://scienceblogs.com/gregladen/2007/11/18/whale-croc-lost-in-brazil.

Launay, Michael J. "Hunting for Capt. Kidd's Buried Treasure." *Asbury Park Press*, August 23, 2014. https://www.app.com/story/news/weird/2014/08/23/hunting-capt-kidds-buried-treasure-new-jersey/14499263.

Lautner, Nina. *Ghosts of America—New Jersey.* N.p.: CreateSpace Independent Publishing Platform, 2016.

Legends of America. "Lenape-Delaware Tribe." https://www.legendsofamerica.com/lenape-delaware-tribe.

Living in the Past. "Colonial Ferry." https://www.living-in-the-past.com/ferry.html.

Loeper, John J. *The Flying Machine: A Stagecoach Journey in 1774.* New York: Atheneum, 1976.

The Lofts at Neilson Crossings. "Congregation Poile Zedek." n.d. https://www.theloftsnb.com.

Longfellow, Rickie. "The Packet Boat—Transportation by Canal." Federal Highway Administration, 2017. https://www.fhwa.dot.gov/infrastructure/back1009.cfm.

Maragoudakis, Peter. "Historic St. Ladislaus Church in New Brunswick Celebrates 110th Anniversary." *New Brunswick Today*, October 20, 2014. https://newbrunswicktoday.com/2014/10/20/historic-st-ladislaus-church-in-new-brunswick-celebrates-110th-anniversary.

Marian, Sara, and Ben M. Marian. "American Hungarian Foundation." Clio: Your Guide to History, 2017. https://theclio.com/entry/41726.

Mathis, Mike. "Spotlight: Middlesex County Courthouse." *Judiciary Times*, 2017. https://www.linkedin.com/pulse/spotlight-middlesex-county-courthouse-njcourts.

Maynard, Barksdale. "The Enigma of the Cannon." *Princeton Alumni Weekly*, 2015. https://paw.princeton.edu/article/enigma-cannon.

McBurney, Christian. "The Battle of Bennett's Island: The New Jersey Site Rediscovered." *Journal of the American Revolution*, 2017. https://allthingsliberty.com/2017/07/battle-bennetts-island-new-jersey-site-rediscovered.

McCloy, James F., and Ray Miller. *Phantom of the Pines: More Tales of the Jersey Devil*. N.p.: Middle Atlantic Press, 1998.

McConaughy, David. "George Janeway (1742–1826)." WikiTree. https://www.wikitree.com/wiki/Janeway-10.

McKenney, Janice E. *Women of the Constitution: Wives of the Signers*. Lanham, MD: Scarecrow Press, 2013.

"Middlesex County Gravestones: The Morris Street Presbyterian Cemetery, New Brunswick." *Genealogical Magazine of NJ* (1999). http://www.nbfplarchive.org/nbrevitalization/files/nb_images/belvin_photos/cemeteries/willow_grove_cemetery/morris_st_presbyterian_cemetery_genealogical_magazine_of_nj_a_1999_01_39_48.pdf.

Mitford, A.B. *Japanese Legends and Folklore: Samurai Tales, Ghost Stories, Legends, Fairy Tales, Myths and Historical Accounts*. North Clarendon, VT: Tuttle Publishing, 2019.

Moran, Mark, and Mark Sceurman. "Cryptic Carvings Along Lawrence Brook." *Weird NJ* (2015). https://weirdnj.com/stories/cryptic-carvings-along-lawrence-brook.

———. "The Final Parking Place of Mary Ellis." *Weird NJ* (2019). https://weirdnj.com/stories/cemetery-safari/mary-ellis-rt-1-parking-lot-grave.

———. "Hunting for the Buried Treasure of Captain Kidd." *Weird NJ* (2021). https://weirdnj.com/stories/mystery-history/captain-kidd.

———. "Joyce Kilmer's 'Tree.'" *Weird NJ*, no. 3 (1992).

Morrison, Zack, dir. *Knights, Tigers, and Cannons. Oh My!* 2012. https://vimeo.com/35066902.

Munoz, Daniel J. "10 Fun Facts You May Not Know About New Brunswick." TAPinto, 2017. https://www.tapinto.net/towns/new-brunswick/sections/arts-and-entertainment/articles/10-fun-facts-you-may-not-know-about-new-bruns.

———. "The Trolleys and Trains That Made New Brunswick the Hub City." *New Brunswick Today*, January 4, 2015. https://newbrunswicktoday.com/2015/01/the-trolleys-and-trains-that-made-new-brunswick-the-hub-city.

Muyskens, Dr. J. David, Reverend. "The Town Clock Church: History of the First Reformed Church New Brunswick, NJ." The Consistory, 1991. https://rucore.libraries.rutgers.edu/rutgers-lib/38779/PDF/1/play.

Nanticoke and Lenape Confederation. "Our Ancient Way of Life." 2017. https://nanticokelenapemuseum.org/museum/1117/our-ancient-way-of-life.

National Park Service. "Thaddeus Kosciuszko National Memorial." https://www.nps.gov/thko/index.htm.

Native American Embassy. "Lenni Lenape Archives: The Masked Being." https://www.nativeamericanembassy.net/www.lenni-lenape.com/www/html/LenapeArchives/LenapeSet-01/mesingw.html.

Nelson, William. *Personal Names of Indians of New Jersey*. Paterson, NJ: Paterson History Club, 1904. https://archive.org/details/personalnamesofi00nels.

Neugroschel, Joachim, ed. *Great Tales of Jewish Occult and Fantasy: The Dybbuk and 30 Other Classic Stories*. Translated by Joachim Neugroschel. N.p.: Wings Books, 1991.

New Brunswick City Center. "History & Tours in New Brunswick City Center." https://www.newbrunswick.com/pub/gen/history-and-tours.

New Brunswick Free Public Library Archives—Digital Archive. http://www.nbfplarchive.org.

New Brunswick Sister Cities Association. "Fukui, Japan." https://www.newbrunswicksistercities.org/projecto-3.

New Jersey Maritime Museum. "Privateers of the Revolutionary War." 2015. https://njmaritimemuseum.org/privateers-of-the-revolutionary-war-part-2.

New York Times. "Rutgers Fraternity House Cloaks a Mystery." May 26, 1929. https://timesmachine.nytimes.com/timesmachine/1929/05/26/91795038.html?pageNumber=55.

New York Tribune. "Psychic 'Prof.' Is Arrested as Witch Doctor." April 22, 1921. https://chroniclingamerica.loc.gov/lccn/sn83030214/1921-04-22/ed-1/seq-1.

Nguyen, Catherine. "Rutgers Seniors Shed Light on Secret Honor Society." *Daily Targum*, October 29, 2018. https://dailytargum.com/article/2018/10/rutgers-seniors-shed-light-on-secret-honor-society.

Offutt, Jason. *Chasing American Monsters: 251 Creatures, Cryptids, and Hairy Beasts*. Woodbury, MN: Llewellyn Publications, 2019.

Oppenheimer, Jerry. *Crazy Rich: Power, Scandal, and Tragedy Inside the Johnson & Johnson Dynasty*. New York: St. Martin's Publishing Group, 2013.

Orczy, Emmuska O. *Old Hungarian Fairy Tales (Illustrated and Unabridged Classic Edition)*. N.p.: CreateSpace Independent Publishing Platform, 2017.

Ortloff, George C. *A Lady in the Lake: The True Account of Death and Discovery in Lake Placid*. Lake Placid, NY: With Pipe and Book, 1985.

PBS. "The Transportation Revolution: Roads, Canals, and Railroads." 2016. https://pbslearningmedia.org/resource/biogam.soc.ush.transrev/transportation-revolution-roads-canals-and-railroads.

PBS American Masters. "Paul Robeson Biography." 2006. https://www.pbs.org/wnet/americanmasters/paul-robeson-about-the-actor/66.

Pfingsten, Bill. "New Brunswick Station Historical Marker." Historical Marker Database. https://www.hmdb.org/m.asp?m=95769.

Powers, Mathew. "First Reformed Church of New Brunswick." Clio: Your Guide to History, 2020. https://theclio.com/entry/100751.

———. "New Brunswick Station." Clio: Your Guide to History, 2020. https://theclio.com/entry/97821.

Railfanning. "Northeast Corridor." https://railfanning.org/history/nec.

Redish, Laura, and Orrin Lewis. "Lenape Language and the Delaware Indian Tribe (Unami, Lenni Lenape)." Native Languages of the Americas. http://www.native-languages.org/lenape.htm.

———. "Native Americans: Algonquian Indians (Algonkian tribe, Algonquians, Algonkians)." Native Languages of the Americas. http://www.bigorrin.org/algonquian_kids.htm.

Regal, Brian, and Frank J. Esposito. *The Secret History of the Jersey Devil: How Quakers, Hucksters, and Benjamin Franklin Created a Monster*. Baltimore, MD: Johns Hopkins University Press, 2019.

Regan, Timothy E. *New Brunswick*. Charleston, SC: Arcadia Publishing Library Editions, 2003.

Roadside America. "Site of Tree from Joyce Kilmer's 'Trees.'" https://www.roadsideamerica.com/story/68666.

Roth, Steven M. "Stage Operations and the Mails in New Jersey." New Jersey Postal History Society, 1972. http://njpostalhistory.org/media/pdf/rothstage.pdf.

Rutgers Alumni. "Scarlet Traditions." https://alumni.rutgers.edu/who-we-are/leadership-boards/scarlet-council/scarlet-traditions.

Rutgers Get Involved. "Cap and Skull Senior Honor Society." CampusLabs. https://rutgers.campuslabs.com/engage/organization/capandskull.

Rutgers Global Health Institute. "New Brunswick Store Owner Gets Help From Equitable Recovery Program." 2021. https://globalhealth.

rutgers.edu/news/new-brunswick-store-owner-gets-help-from-equitable-recovery-program.

Rutgers University. "First Classes Held at Local Tavern." https://timeline.rutgers.edu/#event-first-classes-held-at-local-tavern.

———. "Rutgers' 'Passion Puddle' Among America's Most Romantic College Spots." 2015. https://www.rutgers.edu/news/rutgers-passion-puddle-among-americas-most-romantic-college-spots.

Sanborn Map Company. "New Brunswick, New Jersey (Sheet 8)," May 1886. Includes key, key map, streets and specials index and text. Princeton University Library Digital Maps & Geospatial Data. https://maps.princeton.edu/catalog/princeton-3t945s88w.

Sasaki Associates Inc. "Rutgers University, University-Wide Physical Master Plan." https://www.sasaki.com/projects/rutgers-university-university-wide-physical-master-plan.

Scarlet and Black Research Center. "Will's Way: Campus Namesakes." https://scarletandblack.rutgers.edu/archive/exhibits/show/namesakes/will-s-way.

Schlosser, S.E. *Spooky New Jersey: Tales of Hauntings, Strange Happenings, and Other Local Lore*. Essex, CT: Globe Pequot, 2017.

Sebold, Kimberly R., Sara A. Leach and U.S. Department of the Interior, National Park Service. "Historic Themes and Resources within the New Jersey Coastal Heritage Trail Route." Southern New Jersey and the Delaware Bay, 2005. https://www.nps.gov/parkhistory/online_books/nj2/contents.htm.

Serrili, Ted. "Historic Ghost Tale Lacks a Lively Spirit." *Home News* (New Brunswick), January 28, 1979.

Shea, Jessica, and Ray Brennan. "Rutgers Rarities." Rutgers Rarities & Unexplained Phenomena. https://rutgersrarities.com.

Sister Cities International (SCI). "Kusakabe Taro: the Samurai Connecting New Brunswick and Fukui." 2017. https://sistercities.org/arts-culture/kusakabe-taro-the-samurai-connecting-new-brunswick-and-fukui.

Slesinski, Jason J. *Along the Raritan River: South Amboy to New Brunswick*. Charleston, SC: Arcadia Publishing, 2014.

Sparago, Mary. "Captain Kidd: The Lost Treasure of New Jersey." New Jersey Digest, 2021. https://thedigestonline.com/nj/lost-treasure-of-new-jersey.

Stackhouse, A.M. *The King's Highway, and the Pen[n]sauken Graveyard: A Chapter in the Colonial History of West New Jersey*. Moorestown, NJ: Settle Press, 1905. https://www.loc.gov/item/06024137.

Stamato, Linda. "Rutgers and Princeton: Tradition, Rivalry and the Cannon Wars." NJ.com, September 11, 2012. https://www.nj.com/njv_linda_stamato/2012/09/rutgers_and_princeton_traditio.html.

The State of New Jersey. "A Brief History of the Delaware and Raritan Canal." 2022. https://www.nj.gov/dep/drcc/about-canal/history.

Sullivan, Jeremiah J., and James F. McCloy. "The Jersey Devil's Finest Hour." *New York Folklore Quarterly* 30, no. 3 (September 1974): 232. ProQuest.

Sullivanby Trenton, Joseph F. "From the Rope to the Chair: 3 Centuries of Death (Published 1996)." *New York Times*, June 16, 1996. https://www.nytimes.com/1996/06/16/nyregion/from-the-rope-to-the-chair-3-centuries-of-death.html.

Tamas, Tamas. "Evolution of a Global Community: New Jersey Hungarians in a Trans-National Ethnic Network." *International Journal of Politics, Culture, and Society* 10, no. 4 (Summer 1997): 615–34. https://www.jstor.org/stable/20019912.

Theodore Roosevelt Center. "Railroads." https://www.theodorerooseveltcenter.org/Learn-About-TR/TR-Encyclopedia/Capitalism%20and%20Labor/Railroads.

Thinkery & Verse. "Ghost Hunt: The Hall-Mills Double Homicide." https://www.thinkeryandverse.org/ghost_hunt.html.

Tibbott, Julie. *Members Only: Secret Societies, Sects, and Cults Exposed!* Minneapolis, MN: Zest Books, 2015.

To the Electors of Middlesex. Proponent of the plan to build the county court in New Brunswick. Signed "a Planter." 1793. Rutgers University Libraries Special Collections & University Archives.

To the Inhabitants of Middlesex County. An argument for placing the county courthouse in New Brunswick, rather than Perth Amboy. 1793? Rutgers University Libraries Special Collections & University Archives.

Treuer, Anton. *Atlas of Indian Nations.* New York: National Geographic Books, 2013.

U.S. Army Corps of Engineers. "A History of Steamboats." https://www.sam.usace.army.mil/Portals/46/docs/recreation/OP-CO/montgomery/pdfs/10thand11th/ahistoryofsteamboats.pdf.

Universal Co-Masonry. "Masonic History | The Legend of Enoch." https://www.universalfreemasonry.org/en/history-freemasonry/legend-of-enoch.

University Archives and Records Center. "John Bubenheim Bayard 1738–1807." https://archives.upenn.edu/exhibits/penn-people/biography/john-bubenheim-bayard.

Vehrer, Adél. "Táltos, Witch, Incubus, Succubus and Other Beings in Hungarian Folklore and Mythology." *Civic Review* 14 (Special Issue 2018): 411–23. DOI: 10.24307/psz.2018.0426.

Wall, John P. *The Chronicles of New Brunswick, N.J., 1667–1931.* Morgantown, PA: Higginson Book Company, 1997.

Warner, Susan. "The Family Behind the Company." *New York Times*, April 10, 2005. https://www.nytimes.com/2005/04/10/nyregion/the-family-behind-the-company.html.

Weiss, Jennifer. "As New Brunswick Grows, City's Hungarians Adapt." *New York Times*, July 14, 2006. https://www.nytimes.com/2006/07/14/nyregion/nyregionspecial2/16njhungarian.html.

Wikipedia. "George I of Great Britain." https://en.wikipedia.org/wiki/George_I_of_Great_Britain.

———. "NEC Raritan River Bridge." https://en.wikipedia.org/wiki/Raritan_River_Bridge.

Wilk, Tom. "100 Years of Douglass College." NJ.com, February 22, 2018. https://www.nj.com/inside-jersey/2018/02/the_100-year_journey_of_douglass_college.html.

William Paterson University. "Who Was William Paterson?" https://www.wpunj.edu/about-us/history/williampaterson_bio.html.

Willow Grove Cemetery. "About Willow Grove." New Brunswick Free Public Library Archive. http://www.willowgrove.nbfpl.org/default.asp.

Yokai. "Nukekubi." https://yokai.com/nukekubi.

Zalka, Csenge V. *Dancing on Blades: Rare and Exquisite Folktales from the Carpathian Mountains.* Marion, MI: Parkhurst Brothers Publishers, 2018.

Zeender, Jim. "In Their Own Words: John Adams and Ben Franklin." Pieces of History, 2012. https://prologue.blogs.archives.gov/2012/06/20/in-their-own-words-john-adams-and-ben-franklin-part-i.

ABOUT THE AUTHOR

Mark Neurohr-Pierpaoli is a high school English and history teacher currently working in the vicinity of New Brunswick. He lives in Burlington County, New Jersey, where he operates informative and entertaining historical walking tours during his "summers off."

Visit us at
www.historypress.com
....